Bernard Lonergan's Method and a Medical Doctor's Approach to Healthcare

Bernard Lonergan's Method and a Medical Doctor's Approach to Healthcare

JOHN RAYMAKER

WIPF & STOCK · Eugene, Oregon

BERNARD LONERGAN'S METHOD AND A MEDICAL DOCTOR'S APPROACH TO HEALTHCARE

Copyright © 2021 John Raymaker. All rights reserved. Except for brief quotations in critical publications or reviews, no part of this book may be reproduced in any manner without prior written permission from the publisher. Write: Permissions, Wipf and Stock Publishers, 199 W. 8th Ave., Suite 3, Eugene, OR 97401.

Wipf & Stock
An Imprint of Wipf and Stock Publishers
199 W. 8th Ave., Suite 3
Eugene, OR 97401

www.wipfandstock.com

PAPERBACK ISBN: 978-1-7252-9353-3
HARDCOVER ISBN: 978-1-7252-9354-0
EBOOK ISBN: 978-1-7252-9355-7

02/25/21

Contents

Foreword by Bishop Pierre W. Whalon | vii

List of Abbreviations | xi

Preface | xiii

I. Getting our Bearings: Putting Medical and Evolutionary Issues and Lonergan's Method in Perspective | 1

II. A Brief Overview of the Eight FS and of a GEM-FS Approach to Medicine | 39

III. The First Mediating-Creative Phase in Lonergan's *Method in Theology*: The Roles of the First Four FS in a GEM-FS Approach to Medicine | 44

IV. The Second Mediated-Healing Phase in Lonergan's *Method in Theology*: The Indispensable Roles of the Last Four Functional Specialties in *MiT* | 70

Appendix A | 99

Appendix B | 101

Appendix C | 104

Appendix D | 109

Appendix E | 115

Appendix F | 117

Bibliography | 119

Selective Subject Index | 129

Foreword

By Bishop Pierre W. Whalon

Bernard J. F. Lonergan is considered by many intellectuals to be the finest philosophic thinker of the 20th century.
—*Time Magazine*, April 20, 1970.

Fifty years later, his method is still considered by many as being very pertinent to the twenty-first century. His opus sprawls across twenty-five volumes lovingly published by the University of Toronto Press. There are Lonergan Study Centers on three continents. Books, academic journals, and myriad published articles dedicated to this or that aspect of his thought abound.

Yet, you might ask why you have never heard of him. Lonergan was born in 1904 in Buckingham, Canada, and died in 1984 in Ontario.[1] He entered the Jesuit order in 1922 and, like all Jesuits, had the benefit of a great deal of education. Lonergan, however, even as a student complained to his superior that his courses were not of a high enough standard, which he went on to set for himself. The span of his opus testifies to his wide-ranging in-depth studies not only in theology and philosophy, but also the sciences, mathematics, sociology, and economics. In all these, he remains influential to this day.

Lonergan was very independent, and his lone-wolf status—not belonging to schools of thought or movements—is perhaps another reason he is not as well-known as he should be. As he matured, his life ambition

---

1. One wonders how his work might have fared if he were American, British, or French.

emerged: to help people discover how their mind actually functions, so that they can improve the lot of humanity. In all his writing and teaching, Lonergan always wanted people to be able to think for themselves and find ways to improve our common life.

The great German philosopher Hannah Arendt, in her Gifford Lecture entitled *The Life of the Mind*, made a crucial point about wanting to know:

> To expect truth to come from thinking signifies that we mistake the need to think with the urge to know. Thinking can and must be employed in the attempt to know, but in the exercise of this function it is never itself; it is but the handmaiden of an altogether different enterprise.[2]

Lonergan would agree and he gave much more precision to the pursuit of this "different enterprise." One starts with that urge to know, which all of us experience in one way or another at some point. But the mind once engaged operates in a process, following a method, and this must be experienced and intellectually grasped for the seeker to fully succeed. He called this "the eros of the human spirit."

> The eros of the human spirit is a tidal movement that begins before consciousness, unfolds through sensitivity, intelligence, rational reflection, responsible deliberation, only to find its rest beyond all of these.[3]

Retroactively speaking, one might say that *Insight: A Study of Human Understanding*, originally published in 1957, helps people catch themselves in the act of this tidal movement.[4] *Insight* is a pedagogy to do exactly that. It is not only about the moves from attention to sense, insights that raise questions for judgment, and acts that reflect sound intelligent, rational, and moral reasoning, but just as importantly, it is about the many ways that we often try to dam the tidal movement, so to speak, through various forms of bias, as well as inattention, stupidity, irrational conclusions, and acts of omission as well as commission. Published fourteen years after *Insight*, *Method in Theology* made an even bigger splash at the time. (It remains Lonergan's one book that most people in 2020 would recognize). As soon as it came out, critics maintained that it was not especially theological, and not even Christian at that. But Lonergan had a deeper, unifying goal in mind. He wanted to help people discover the deeper aspects of their own consciousness. He

---

2. Arendt, *Life of the Mind*, 1:61. She was the first woman to be invited to this prestigious lecture series.

3. Lonergan, "Natural Right," 175.

4. Lonergan, *Insight*, 1997.

suggested ways "self-appropriated" persons can join to accomplish all the myriad tasks of understanding that humans can undertake so as to change the world for the better.

Patrick Daly, MD, has used the insights of Bernard Lonergan to improve the practice of medicine by clarifying the way practitioners think—beginning with their urge to know—when seeking to ail their patients. In a series of important articles, he attacks the many failings of modern medical systems that have lost or have never had the proper focus on the patient. While it might seem that Lonergan's thinking is abstract and remote from such realities, it is in fact totally centered on the concrete. Dr. Daly deftly applies it to help practitioners understand and correct the many ills of the system the only way that can realistically happen: by seeking to change the views physicians have of themselves.

John Raymaker is one of the world's leading thinkers applying Lonergan's thought to contemporary challenges, and a conversation partner with Patrick Daly. In eleven previous books, Raymaker has addressed interreligious dialogue (he is an expert in Japanese Buddhism), climate change, overcoming biases in science and philosophy, issues in the Roman Catholic Church, and introducing Lonergan's thought itself. Raymaker did not coin the expression "generalized empirical method" (GEM) on which *Insight* is based, but he makes a breakthrough in coupling GEM as a *generalized* method with the functional *specialization* (FS) method featured in *Method in Theology*.[5] The present volume pivots on "GEM-FS," a rather succinct and helpful way of combining the *generalized* and *specialized* aspects of Lonergan's transcendental method. Raymaker addresses the importance of the Lonerganian "GEM model" that Daly has advocated for healthcare and medicine over the past few years, but he also seeks to move that GEM model into a second, wider horizon that includes the pivotal, integrative roles of the FS.

Daly limits himself mostly to *Insight*. As monumental and perennially relevant as *Insight* is, in reality, the later Lonergan continued to explore the implications of his theory. This led him to focus on functional specialization as noted above—it amounts to his having embarked on a major shift. Whereas *Insight* still bears the marks of his scholastic training—from which he had begun to distance himself—in *Method in Theology* and other later works, Lonergan developed an even more revolutionary approach. Building on that which "unfolds through sensitivity, intelligence, rational reflection, responsible deliberation,"[6] he began to emphasize more that the *process* of

---

5. Lonergan, *MiT*, 1972.
6. Lonergan, "Natural Right," 175. Bishop Pierre W. Whalon was bishop in charge of

how persons come to know and to act can and should be applied to the *processes* of community life so as to have a common basis across the globe to tackle social inequalities, climate change, etc.

Let me explain. It is a truism that "no man is an island." We need each other in order for all our needs to be met, and to contribute toward meeting the needs of others—no one can long survive alone. Lonergan had already realized in *Insight* that his method is applicable to communities as well as to individuals. In *Method in Theology*, Lonergan stresses this latter point—thereby transposing the four basic differentiations of consciousness of his generalized empirical method to the eight stages of the "functional specialties," namely research, interpretation, history, dialectic, and foundations, doctrines, systematics, and communications. The FS outline the "tidal movements" that can sweep through a community when various people pay attention to a phenomenon and describe it; figuring out where it came through valid forms of argumentation. Then as arguments are contrasted, the dialectic eventually resolves in a higher viewpoint, "foundations," which is then described, explained, and finally communicated to the world.

Raymaker's GEM-FS shorthand focuses on and integrates the overall dimensions of Lonergan's work, while making suggestions as to how these dimensions could be more effectively applied to Daly's GEM model which only goes "halfway" in applying Lonergan's method to health care. Raymaker does consider Daly's accomplishment so significant that he seeks to complete the circle by transposing Daly's insights into a potentially interactive GEM-FS "tidal-wave" process at the service of humanity.

Bernard Lonergan's Method and a Medical Doctor's Approach to Healthcare is a must-read not only for medical professionals, but also for anyone interested in improving medical care. The book will be useful to those who want to know what "the finest philosophic thinker of the 20th century" can bring to bear on today's many pressing threats to humanity's survival—a process that functions in concrete situations.

---

the Convocation of Episcopal Churches in Europe from 2001 to 2019.

List of Abbreviations

ACS	American Society for Cybernetics
AIRR	the transcendental precepts, be attentive; be intelligent; be reasonable; be responsible, emphasized in *Insight*, can be reduplicatively reprised in inverse order as occurs in *MiT*.
COVID-19	Corona Virus Disease 2019
CWL	*Collected Works of Lonergan*
DNA	Deoxyribonucleic acid composed of two polynucleotide chains that form a double helix
FS	Functional Specialties of Functional Specialization used by Lonergan in *Method in Theology* and later Works
GEM	Generalized Empirical Method
GEM-FS	Generalized Empirical Method Functionally Specialized
GST	General Systems Theory
MiT	*Method in Theology*
mRNA	Messenger RNA. A single-stranded molecule of RNA that corresponds to the genetic sequence of a gene
RNA	Ribonucleic acid: a polymeric molecule essential in coding and decoding genes
RS	Recurrent Schemes
WES	Whole Exome Sequencing
WGS	Whole Genome Sequencing
WHO	World Health Organization

Preface

This book seeks to show that Bernard Lonergan's method, primarily meant to answer the many problems that have traditionally affected philosophy and theology, can also be applied both to healthcare and medicine as well as to broader topics such as evolution. My aim is to situate a series of articles by Patrick Daly, MD—which seek to apply Lonergan's method to healthcare—within a larger perspective. For example, Daly refers to Lonergan's important article "Healing and Creating in History,"[1] only tangentially. I refer to it in more detail with a view to further enlarge Daly's arguments. In his "Healing and Creating" article, Lonergan alludes to his own study of human biases; biases poison human relationships. He also makes it a point to stress the greed of multinational corporations whose main aim is to maximize profits.

Human greed and biases point to a need to come to terms with the implications of evolutionary realities as well with the psychic elements of human life. I hope to show that Daly's proposal, although sound, should be broadened to include Lonergan's original approach to functional-specialization (FS) in *Method in Theology* (*MiT*).[2] This includes the roles of the biases and one's presuppositions—especially as these influence a thinker's approach to the last four functional specialties. That means that in human studies, while one must first focus on the past before addressing the future, there are crucial transition points in doing so. One must identify these transition

---

1. Lonergan, "Healing and Creating in History," 100–109.

2. Lonergan, *MiT*. Halse, *Lonergan's Methodology*, suggests ways in which functional specialization can contribute to inquires into religious diversity. I shall argue that uses of functional specialization (FS) can be extended beyond the domain of theology to include e. g. societal-ethical-medical issues.

points, if one is to properly account for the complexity of our human situation. In the case of Daly, for example, he would have done well to dwell more on the communal aspects of medicine as this has been influenced by, for example, evolutionary realities. Lonergan's FS approach is derived from his earlier study of the four levels of human cognitional-doing activities in *Insight*.[3] Below I strive to link Lonergan's publications, which touch on many complex topics, with studies in human evolution and with the challenges we face in our in an age of globalization. It is important to note how Lonergan kept on enlarging his perspectives throughout his career. In this respect, one may compare how Lonergan constantly broadened his perspectives with how, in their own faith-based visionary writings, Teilhard de Chardin and Pope[4] Francis have addressed the implications of evolution.

Lonergan focused more on scientific methods in general than on the practice of particular sciences. To the extent that he did write on evolution he was concerned more about the implications of scientific method than on giving an account of evolution based on Darwinism[5] or neo-Darwinism. Serious thinkers cannot ignore the complexities of today's world. Too often, when we hear the words "global crisis" we tend to focus on the word "crisis" rather than on "global." The coronavirus pandemic that has affected all humans, irrespective of race or religion, means that in a globalized world, we need a method that can effectively address and interrelate the human, social dysfunctions that have led to various types of planetary and human crises.[6]

---

3. Originally published in 1953, Lonergan's *Insight* is available in *Collected Works*, vol. 3.

4. See, for example, Raymaker and Grudzen, *Pope Francis, Conscience*. Byrne, "Evolutionary Science," shows how Lonergan's philosophy of science can help resolve the controversy between Intelligent Design theorists and proponents of neo-Darwinian evolution. Intelligent Design theories argue that the complex structures of living organisms cannot be adequately explained by neo-Darwinian theories, especially in the latter's postulate of random variations. Hence, an "intelligent designer" must be postulated in order to fill out scientific explanations. Byrne finds fault with some Intelligent Design arguments; he proposes a different approach—one that accepts neo-Darwinian evolution (or something very much like it). He shows how Lonergan's analysis of scientific methods grounds his account of evolution, and how much this can overcome the most basic Intelligent Design objections. He then shows how Lonergan's philosophy of God offers a design argument based, not in the complexity of this or that organism, but in the "design" of evolution itself. I argue that GEM-FS is an apt, inclusive way for realizing Byrne's argument.

5 While the term Darwinism is still used by the general public, it is now deemed an inappropriate designation of modern evolutionary theory.

6. The phrase "Man's inhumanity to man" was used in Robert Burns's poem, "Man was made to mourn" in 1784. Possibly, Burns reworded a Samuel von Pufendorf quote; in 1673, Pufendorf wrote, "More inhumanity has been done by man himself than by any other of nature's causes."

I aim, in this book, to reach beyond Daly's use of a "GEM model" so as to include the personal commitments and/or conversions outlined in Lonergan's two-phase or "diphase method"[7] which is at the core of his method in later publications.

---

7. Lonergan, *MiT*, 133, indicates that "if one encounters the past, one also has to take one's stand toward the future." This becomes the basis of his mediating and mediated phases in theology, which I paraphrase as his "diphase method."

1

Getting our Bearings

Putting Medical and Evolutionary Issues and Lonergan's Method in Perspective

The published articles of Patrick Daly, MD, seek to show the relevance of Bernard Lonergan's *Insight* by "fleshing out the model and the generic levels of human living."[1] Daly's work is important and relevant, but it is limited to suggesting how Lonergan's extraordinary "generalized empirical method" (GEM) can help remedy some of the dysfunctional aspects in modern healthcare and medicine which include such facts that in the United States:

- Many people are not receiving the right care at the right time.
- In actual practice, not enough focus is given on preventative healthcare.
- The healthcare system is geared toward reactive sick-care; the system tends to prod patients to seek medical attention only when they are already in a state of ill health.
- A lack of preventative healthcare; this often results in people developing chronic conditions that could have been avoided.[2]

My aim in this book is twofold:

---

1. Daly, "GEM Model," 421—later amplified in other issues of that periodical.
2. See "What Is Wrong."

1. To examine Daly's imaginative, detailed and original proposal of "a GEM model" in some detail, but

2. To point out that his published articles—mostly centered on Lonergan's GEM as developed in *Insight*, have not drawn the full implications of Lonergan's method. Such implications require focusing on such processes as personal, communal, social developments.

These implications, drawn out by Lonergan himself in his *Method in Theology* (*MiT*), *can and should be* applied as was done, for example, in a book I co-authored with Ijaz Durrani addressing today's climate change crises.[3] We outlined how Lonergan's approach to functional specialization is admirably suited to help humanity find solutions to deal with the alarming rise of temperatures across the planet. Unlike Daly, Durrani and I stressed, as does Lonergan in *MiT*, the need of two phases to fully apply Lonergan's generalized *and* specialized method to contemporary problems.

The fact that Daly has not explored in needed detail Lonergan's stress on functional specialization (FS) in *MiT* means that he has not identified the full relevance of Lonergan's lifework. Fifteen years separate the publication of Lonergan's two major works. Within that timeframe, Lonergan was exploring many challenges and dilemmas facing humanity. For example, Lonergan, in 1959, refers to Albert Einstein who had complained that "it was impossible to be intelligent" in the modern world so as to communicate a grasp of the whole. "Intelligence is a very delicate plant, requiring favorable circumstances in which to develop. Einstein does not believe it can survive under the present set up of university curricula."[4]

Placing Daly's Commendable Focus on a Patient's Experience within a More Inclusive GEM-FS-Process Approach[5]

In one article, Daly concludes that

3. Raymaker and Durrani, *Empowering* stresses, as I do here, that the eight FS can be used in all disciplines.

4. Lonergan, *Topics in Education*, 17.

5. Lonergan's "GEM-FS-process approach" is based on his integration of the data of sense and those of consciousness. It is noteworthy that the French philosophers Henri Bergson and Michel Foucault also had "process approaches" to history, philosophy, and decision-making. Their works give some parameters for my attempting to situate Daly's work within a more inclusive GEM-FS-process approach. I have developed analogous approaches to GEM-FS in, e.g., my *Third Way*, which explores the differences between some of the technical and religious templates for bridging spiritual and secular approaches to modern complexities. Secularists today make it methodologically difficult to appeal to a loving God in daily life and to devise ecumenical, interfaith strategies.

> The clinical encounter, as the hub of healthcare, is an example of the self-correcting cycle of learning in action, which in this case revolves around the patient's experience of health and illness. The clinician attends to the patient's illness in the mode of subject-as-object and seeks to understand the patient's illness in terms of disease in the mode of subject-to-object. The patient experiences and seeks to understand illness in the mode of subject-as-subject as well as subject-as-object; like the clinician, the patient may also seek to understand illness in terms of disease in the mode of subject-to-object. Clinician and patient attempt to move from a commonsense to an explanatory perspective and then back again as this affects the narrative of the patient's life. This interaction involves another mode of conscious intentionality, subject-to-subject. . . . . In a clinical context, ongoing attention to transcendental method promises to deepen our understanding of personal relations at the basis of health science and practice.[6]

Yes, Daly is right. This "domain" merits further investigation. I shall argue that Lonergan's method is not only a *generalized* empirical method but it is one that is also functionally *specialized* (GEM-FS). That is, *Insight* laid the *generalized* ground upon which Lonergan later developed in *MiT* a method for *specialized* collaboration. I aim to transpose Daly's original contribution to GEM studies so as to "plug it in" within each of the eight FS—thereby amplifying-while-*transposing* the scope of Daly's original contribution to GEM studies.[7] Even though, Lonergan applied GEM-FS mainly to philosophy and theology, I shall argue that Daly's "GEM model" can and should be extended to GEM-FS' two phases[8] if his aim is to comprehensively address healthcare or the practice of medicine. My "process-revision" of Daly's model is not a "put-down." Rather, it is an effort do draw out in more depth the potential that Daly has discovered in Lonergan's method. It is a praise-critique, or a critical appraisal, as it were, of Daly's efforts. Ironically, Daly's intention is to show how Lonergan's method presents

> A unique framework—a higher viewpoint—for integrating the manifold viewpoints of clinical practice and . . . the humanities

---

6. Daly, "Transcendental Method in Action," 7.

7. Since my doctorate is not in medicine, but in social ethics, I rely on medical experts in each FS before applying their expertise from philosophical-ethical perspectives in each of the eight FS.

8. Functional specialization attends to field specialization in the first mediating-creative phase and to subject specialization in the second mediated-healing phase, It then relates them dynamically. See Lonergan, *MiT*, 125, and Tracy, *Achievement*, 262.

(the drama and narrative of human living), health science and health policy in a methodically dynamic and critically progressive fashion in order to address the many pressing problems of contemporary healthcare.[9]

Yet, one cannot overlook the fact that the later Lonergan saw the need to develop his "unique framework" to *include the radically different approaches to past realities and future possibilities*[10] in addressing human situations. He did so, for example, by appealing to God's gift of his love[11] which opens a person's horizons and re-orients the exercise of one's liberty in relation to God, ourselves and neighbor. As is the case with the question of God himself, re-orienting one's self is fundamentally a matter of interiority.

Realistically, one must with Lonergan insist on grasping a "unity, identity, whole in data." This unity "is grasped, not by considering data from an abstractive viewpoint, but by taking them in their concrete individuality and in the totality of their aspects."[12] We can do this despite the limitations of our intelligence. For Lonergan, "models stand to the human sciences, to philosophies, to theologies, much as mathematics stands to the natural sciences."[13] In this context, Lonergan does not refer to medicine which he regards as an applied science.[14]

---

9. Daly, "GEM Model," abstract. Daly has used his long experience and concern with end-of-life and death issues. Daly, "Possibility of Hope," 59–84, asks what is the relation of grace and nature in terms of development. He argues that development from above is linked with the higher levels of our conscious intentionality when these initiate corresponding developments on lower levels. He stresses the operational vector—the functional interdependence of human development—that can be correlated with the functions of our conscious intentionality. He interprets this as "the possibility of hope" which brings forth a new energy and efficacy in all goodness for the rest of our lives. "Possibility of Hope" is a wonderful, very insightful article which anticipates many of my arguments in this book but which I argue Daly could, should have pursued more systematically in terms of all eight FS.

10. Technically this involves the notions of horizons and moving viewpoints in Lonergan's work which underlie and reinforce his views on developmental processes manifested, e.g., in his distinction between faith and beliefs. As in the previous footnote, I stress that Daly's "Possibility of Hope" was on the right track in interrelating God's working in our lives.

11. Lonergan, *MiT*, 103.

12. Lonergan, *Insight*, 271.

13. Lonergan, *MiT*, 284.

14. For the record, I stress that I first asked Dr. Daly to join me in extending his work to include the FS. He replied that he was "too busy" for such an endeavor. This left me in the delicate situation of being unable to directly engage with him in the type of functional-specialization efforts Lonergan stresses in *MiT*—even though I had called Daly's attention to such a need.

In his various articles, Daly has tended to overlook how the later Lonergan developed GEM's larger implications which clearly calls for *a two-phase (diphase) GEM-FS approach*. Daly, has indeed made good use of many systemic[15] relations that can be understood in terms of a unified set of insights, but, paradoxically, he has not drawn out the full implications of the later Lonergan's own contributions to systemic-systematic relations spelled out not only in *MiT*, but also in his "Healing and Creating in History."[16] My intention is to extend Daly's proposal by addressing both planetary and human dysfunctions using Lonergan's eightfold FS method. Daly rightly criticizes the Cartesian presuppositions that underlie some current medical models such as an ontological dualism of mind and matter. Denying any real difference between mind and matter amounts to materialism. Daly rejects the notion that organisms are machines, an analogy that Descartes considered in his *Discourse on Method*,[17] and that still informs much contemporary biological thinking based on engineering or technological principles. Such a viewpoint discounts the difference in kind between non-living and living things, independent of a further differentiation of being at the levels of consciousness and reflective intelligence.

Part of Daly's intent is to try to bridge cartesian dualism with a more differentiated account that would relate and integrate the different levels of human conscious operations. As Daly rightly says, this has both epistemic and ontological implications. It is important to make these implications explicit.[18] In my previous work, beginning with my PhD thesis on the theory-praxis of social ethics,[19] I have focused on systemic relations inherent in

---

15. It is important to note the difference between systemic and systematic. "Systemic" entered the English language in the early 1800s some two hundred years after "systematic." Systemic was first coined by doctors to describe something that happens or exists throughout a whole biological system such as the whole nervous system or even a patient's entire body. Doctors speak, for example, of someone having a systemic infection. I address systemic-systematic differences in FS 7.

16. Lonergan, "Healing and Creating," 100–112.

17 Descartes, "Discourse on the Method," 111–51.

18. Damasio's *Error* and Frattaroli's *Healing* both perceptively address the need for a philosophical grounding of medicine's approach to the human brain that includes psychotherapy to aid patients.

19. Since I approach GEM-FS from ethical viewpoints, I call attention to the interrelationships among the three levels of ethics, and how these levels interrelate with other disciplines and the concrete praxis of everyday life. The first level of ethics, or practical morality, is the level of moral rules or imperatives. It deals with the application of particular moral codes. The second level deals with the basic question of the ground or essence of what makes an action "good." This level also tries to integrate moral imperatives or rules into coherent systems. The third or meta-ethical level investigates the very presuppositions that inform the various ethical theories (second level) behind

such fields as interdisciplinary studies, interfaith dialogue, and the foundations of spirituality. In these endeavors, I have suggested ways whereby Lonergan's eight functional specialties (FS) outlined in *MiT* can be applied in many such fields. Here again, I wish to stress how GEM-FS can indeed help humanity solve some of its problems in various areas of life—if carried out in full *diphase* GEM-FS fashion rather than in what I call Daly's "mere single-phase" GEM-model approach. This means that Lonergan's transcendental method should be implemented as a generalized two-phase feedback *process* at the heart of our human knowing-doing operations.[20] This generalized "self-correcting" GEM-FS feedback process is at the core of Lonergan's overall achievement as, e.g., depicted in Figure 1's illustration of *MiT*'s two interactive mediating-mediated phases.

Daly correctly notes that Lonergan's method is generalized in two ways relative to empirical and phenomenological methods:

> First, it attends to both data of sense (colors, sounds, odors, tastes, the wet and the dry and so forth) and to data of consciousness (acts of seeing, hearing, smelling, tasting, perceiving, imagining, inquiring . . .). So-called subjective data are not assigned a secondary status, as per Galileo and Locke, and acts of intelligence are not cut off from acts of sensibility, as per Kant.
>
> Second, generalized empirical method generalizes the notion of method. "It wants to go behind the diversity that separates the experimental method of the natural sciences and the quite diverse procedures of hermeneutics and of history. It would discover their common core and thereby prepare the way for their harmonious combination in human studies.[21]

One should add, however, that Lonergan's GEM-FS method is not merely a *generalized* empirical one; it is one that is also functionally *specialized* in eight interrelated, interactive functions. Ideally, GEM-FS can guide communities of inquirers to collaborate in effective ways. In my view, Daly's praiseworthy focus on the human good, as in Figure 2, stands in need of a more thorough application of Lonergan's method by systematically interlinking the eight functional specialties. GEM-FS can be used not only to study *human dysfunctions* but also to help remedy these dysfunctions

---

particular patterns of behavior (first level). See Werkmeister, *Theories of Ethics*, 7.

20. This generalized feedback process has to be correlated with the "reduplicative feedback" potential inherent in *MiT*'s two phases. See Figure 1. It may be said that the coronavirus pandemic now raging throughout the world requires global cooperation—that is, a process approach extensively developed in MiT's GEM-FS diphase formula.

21. Daly, "GEM Model," 421–42..

as Lonergan strove to do. Some argue that it is modern dysfunctions that have led to, e.g., the planetary COVID-19 pandemic.[22] Seeking to draw out the fuller implications and relevance of Lonergan's work, Figure 1 outlines the *reduplicative feedback* process[23] inherent in GEM-FS—a process that can help foster systemic cooperation in all human endeavors. Like Daly, I seek to integrate systemic medical practices within evolutionary processes. But I shall transpose some of his arguments for evolutionary and molecular biology[24] *so as to enrich his one-phase approach* to GEM with the processes that occur in nature and in our own psychic, intellectual operations. I say "one-phase" because Daly does not draw the full implications of Lonergan's insistence on the two phases at the core of his *Method in Theology*.

Daly's One-Phase GEM Version of Lonergan's Method

Daly's aim is to develop "a comprehensive model of health based on Bernard Lonergan's philosophy"[25] within contemporary efforts to understand the relation between the health science and healthcare. He had previously explored the philosophical background of his proposed GEM model before comparing it to other accounts of health and disease. For Daly, his model is part of an ongoing project which is in contrast to the dialectical orientation of his earlier papers in which he had analyzed several mainstream accounts

22. Audrey Tan writes that "Climate change may have some bearing on the way the world responds to the COVID-19 pandemic, even though it may not have directly caused it . . . Climate change may affect some of the factors in the COVID-19 equation while placing additional stress on health systems . . . Water, for example, is used for personal hygiene, medical care, drinking and food production. But its availability could be affected by climate change, which can cause erratic rainfall and drought." (Tan, "Climate Change," paras. 1–3).

23. On reduplicative GEM-FS feedback process, see Raymaker, *Empowering Bernard Lonergan's Legacy*, 89, 93 where I suggest that the word "reduplicative" that normally refers to the simple repetition of sounds such as in "okey-dokey" could be expanded with nuances implied in Lonergan's diphase method. To put rather facetiously, the okay or okey is reinforced with dokey's consensus. It is not a mere blanket agreement; dokey implies a reflexive process conceding the reality of another's assessment with a view to hopefully "move on" by opening some quite new perspectives.

24. See also McShane's *Core Precepts* that refers to new kinds of supramolecular and combinatorial chemistry, as well as to evolutionary molecular engineering—all methods for developing better super-molecules. Lonergan was not unaware of developments in chemistry and other sciences that had some bearing on his writing *MiT* and on his relating God's infinity to the ways humans interact in intersubjective ways.

25. Daly, "GEM Model," 422. Lonergan was not primarily a philosopher, but rather a methodologist who wrote on the need to find a modern way to write about theology. Having studied the scientific method in *Insight* and other writings he devised an original method that *can be* applied beyond the field of theology.

in bioethics.²⁶ He insists that his later efforts are "foundational." He quotes Lonergan's observation that "models stand as foundational to the human sciences in much the same way that mathematics stands to the natural sciences. For models purport to be, not descriptions of reality, not hypotheses about reality, but simply interlocking sets of terms and relations."²⁷ They orient investigation as a sketch to be filled out or as a clue to what might be overlooked as currently formulated; they also facilitate description and communication regarding complex realities. Daly proposes to lay out a basic set of terms and relations that

> can serve as a methodically dynamic framework for understanding health science and healthcare practice that is relevant to clinicians, researchers, educators, policy makers, those engaged in cultural critique . . . and in the final analysis to any thoughtful person.²⁸

With respect to cultural critique, Daly's project is meant to systematically relate the manifold problems currently addressed by philosophies of medicine, philosophies of psychiatry, philosophies of nursing, "bioethics, medical humanities, and related subdisciplines."²⁹ Daly stresses that his is a model of health rather than a medical model, and that "in an important sense" his is "also definitely an ecological model."³⁰ Still his "ecological" model fails to fully incorporate Lonergan's diphase approach to GEM-FS outlined in *Method in Theology*. More to the point, he under-emphasizes the fact that Lonergan speaks of GEM-FS *as more than* furnishing mere *clues* to the realities of nature, including human nature which *are both ongoing processes*; COVID-19, for example, has upended human life throughout the globe. Daly tells us that he hopes to demonstrate that GEM "provides a way to integrate health-related theory and practice and, within the realm of theory, to coordinate the role of natural and human science in a unified health science."³¹ His model relies in part on Lonergan's theory of emergent probability:

26. Daly, "Common Sense," 187–203; Daly, "Palliative Sedation," 197–213, (2015).

27. Lonergan, *MiT*, 284. Yet, on page xii of *MiT*, Lonergan insists that he is offering "more then mere models."

28. Daly, "Concise Guide," 966. On the other hand, Lonergan, *MiT*, 285, specifies that such "models will be built up from basic terms and relations that refer to transcultural components in human living and operation," that is they are derivative, based on psychic, cognitional processes. Lonergan himself specifies that is it is "up to the theologian to decide whether any model is to become an hypothesis or to be taken as a description."

29. Daly, "Concise Guide," 966.

30. Daly, "Concise Guide," 966, refers to Sulmasy, "Biopsychosocial," 24–33.

31. Daly, "GEM Model," abstract: Daly refers to Lonergan, *Insight*, 146–51. Yet, note that in *Insight*, 250–55, Lonergan delves into the social surd and human biases and

The stratification and probabilistic interrelation of generically distinct levels of function within organisms as well as the world within which organisms live and die. Furthermore, the model relies on Lonergan's account of the structure of the human good as a key to relating the historical and natural dimensions of human living. Generalized empirical method, emergent probability, and the structure of the human good constitute the three legs on which the GEM model of health stands."[32]

I shall argue that these "three legs" can be considered as two overarching components since emergent probability and GEM are both generalized feedback *processes* while the structure of the human good outlined in *MiT* is part of Lonergan's effort to assemble "the various components that enter into the human good."[33] As noted in Appendix F (and Figure 2) on "The Human Good," these various components include skills, feeling, values, beliefs, cooperation, and decline."[34] My aim is to complement, while enlarging within a broader, encompassing perspective Daly's GEM model of health with a GEM-FS process approach, one mindful of the later Lonergan's *reduplicative-feedback* way[35] to devise an encompassing interdisciplinary, eightfold FS method for the good of humanity. A GEM-FS process approach can do much more than just provide "clues." It is an ideal method for coordinating the work of communities of inquirers—but this would require further efforts on the part of Lonergan experts.[36] GEM-FS process has to be implemented. It goes far beyond giving possible clues which are sources of insight. It has both a wider reach and would be more effective in coordinating breakthroughs in ongoing societal processes and/or in endowing these with an ethical-spiritual grounding. "The interlocking set of terms and relations" which informs Daly's model, should, I argue, not be taken merely as clues but as dynamic sets informing potentially effective actions to address the systemic realities and/or distortions humans are called upon

---

insists that the human sciences have to be critical in rejecting mechanist determinism.

32. Daly, "GEM Model," 423. On the human good, Lonergan, *MiT*, 48, and Figure 2 in Appendix F.

33. Lonergan, *MiT*, 27.

34. Lonergan, *MiT*, 27.

35. Doran, "Complicate," argues that a "reduplicative structure similar to that which accounts for the explicitation" of the FS is involved in Lonergan's accounting for the scale of values which is based on "the increasing degrees of self-transcendence to which one is carried in one's response to values at the different levels." I, too, include this scale as being an integral part of GEM-FS process.

36. I have developed this theme in Raymaker, *Empowering Bernard Lonergan's Legacy*, and in other publications.

to confront. Lonergan defines method as "a set of related and recurrent operations cumulatively advancing towards an ideal goal."[37] Inasmuch as it is specialized, GEM-FS is to be conceived, "not as a single set of related operations but a series of interdependent sets."[38] It distinguishes and separates stages of the process from data to results. It is a matter of a *single process* of investigation being divided into successive stages. It can also be relevant, I argue, in integrating medicine and psychic processes[39] within evolutionary perspectives.

Daly distances himself from Engel's biopsychosocial model (BPS) which in the 1980s became a landmark event for understanding medicine as a science. BPS prompted a revolution in medical thinking by providing an argument and rationale that seemed to better link medicine to science. BPS claimed to be an interdisciplinary model that looks at the interconnection between biology, psychology, and socio-environmental factors. It examined how these aspects play a role in topics ranging from health and disease models to human development. But the BPS model was soon discarded as insufficient,[40] even though it did stress that our contemporary globalized, secularized civilization is in need of a fundamental rethinking of cultural and interdisciplinary issues today.

Daly points to the ideological, insufficient nature of the BPS model, but the GEM alternative he offers does not go far enough. He is on the scent of Lonergan's achievement as applicable to the field of medicine, but he neglects some core insights Lonergan developed in *MiT*, especially the importance of

---

37. Lonergan, *MiT*, 125. Lonergan, *MiT*, xi, insists that his model is that of a "dynamic structure" that one can discover for oneself.

38. Lonergan, *MiT*, 125.

39. Doran, *Dialectics of History*, 59, defines psychic conversion as a "transformation of the psychic component of what Freud calls 'the censor from a repressive to a constructive agency in a person's development. The habitual orientation of our intelligence and affectivity exercises a censorship over the emergence into consciousness of the images that are the psychic representation and conscious integration of an underlying neural manifold. But that censorship can be either constructive or repressive." It is "constructive when one wants a needed insight and so is open to the emergence of the images required for that insight." It is repressive when one does not want the insight and so excludes from consciousness the images required if the unwanted insight is to emerge. . . ..Since the images are easier to repress than the feeling, the affective component becomes dissociated from its imaginal apprehensive correspondent, and attaches itself to other and incongruous images." The result is "a progressive fragmentation of sensitive consciousness." (cf. *Insight*, 181–206).

40. Nassir Ghaemi, *Rise and Fall*, rejects the eclectic nature of the BPS model in favor of a pluralistic, method-based approach to psychiatry. With Daly, I seek in Lonergan's work on the nature of values a sounder scientific basis to include addressing the issue of planetary healing.

the two pivotal mediating-mediated phases underpinning the conversions. By overlooking these key developmental aspects of Lonergan's work, he, in effect, shortchanges his own goal. My intent is to rely on the two phases of Lonergan's transcendental method as applied in the eight FS of *MiT*'s diphase process approach to transpose Daly's "three legs" into a process methodology. My intention is not to "oppose" Daly's claims for GEM as applicable to medicine but to invite him to go further. I shall argue that *MiT* stresses the need to develop two phases that would apply, for example, to accounts of practicing medicine which Lonergan calls "an applied science."[41] The two phases provide the *indispensable pivot that enable the feedback nature* of GEM-FS as rooted in the basic operations all humans use in coming to know and in living their lives. I invite the reader to probe more deeply into Lonergan's fuller treatment of our knowing-doing operations than Daly has. Let me here cite two passages where Lonergan stresses the foundational process that grounds his method. The first touches on the important difference between the uses of method in the sciences and in philosophy:

> Empirical method leaves the sciences open to radical revision, because its appeal is to the data of sense but its basic terms and relations denote not the data of sense but constructs derived from empirically established laws. In contrast, the basic terms and relations of an empirically established cognitional theory are not just constructs but also data of immediate consciousness. Its basic terms denote conscious events. Its basic relations denote stages in conscious process.[42]

Secondly, in *MiT*, Lonergan explains that our knowing-doing operations stand within a process that is formally dynamic, one that calls forth and assembles its own components. It

> does so intelligently, rationally, responsibly. Such, then, is the unity and relatedness of the several operations. It is a unity and relatedness that exists and functions before we manage to advert to it explicitly, understand it, objectify it. It is a unity and relatedness quite different from the intelligible unities and relations by which we organize the data of sense, for they are merely

---

41. Lonergan, *Topics in Education*, 76. See also Morelli and Morelli, *Lonergan Reader*, 27.

42. Lonergan, "Aquinas Today," 47. The "derived constructs" are based on both types of data. The use of both basic terms and basic relations underpin and enable both of *MiT*'s interactive mediating-mediated phases.

intelligible, while the unity and relatedness of conscious process is intelligent, reasonable, responsible.[43]

Two important points in these quotes are Lonergan's stressing the dynamic *process* of knowing and how the data of sense differ from the data of consciousness. The latter are not merely intelligible, they are intelligent. They form a pattern, a *process* of intelligent inquiry leading to results. In the overall Lonergan corpus, the intelligible-intelligent nature of the operations is an instance of what enabled him to transcend, for example, such limited views as those of BPS. The process of intelligent inquiry also lies at the base of the *partially insightful* argument Daly makes concerning Lonergan's approach to emergent probability. Daly notes[44] that Lonergan's theory of emergent probability implies that, given large numbers of events and long periods of time, it is probable that schemes of recurrence may set the stage for more elaborate schemes to follow. This theory serves as the basis for both the stability and the evolution of the universe, considered as intelligible and as supporting the development of intelligence. Evolution involves a series of processes that GEM-FS elaborates on—both as to their occurrence and as to how scientists address them.[45]

How Daly's GEM Model of Health Improves on the Biopsychosocial Model

In his "GEM Model of Health," Daly discusses background issues of method that underlie his model, which is based on Lonergan's account of emergent probability. The latter is a "differentiated and developmental worldview that stands in sharp contrast to inadequately differentiated viewpoints of

---

43. Lonergan, *MiT*, 16. The poet and engineer, Lina Ru (http://beingpoetry.com/perception/) has a very poetic way of describing our knowing process. She writes: "Thinking about texts as precise pieces that communicate exact meaning is based on false assumptions which in turn create a false rationality. Rationality isn't rational because rationality is a consequence of play thought. We assume that rationality is serious play though, but is it? Rationality is dependent on our ability to create and to assume correctly. Assume incorrectly and the created won't be truth, it will be an interpretation not of the truth, but the person who expresses such truth. . . . It is the truth for them as they assume what is needed for it to be true. The only way to arrive to Truth is to allow the play of thought to be as creative as it can be to the point that creativity becomes a process of creative love, a kind of selfless creativity. This process is sometimes referred as the 'creative flow.' A moment is space where there is no 'me', but the process of being one with what is being created. Artists and scientists well know about this creative process."

44. Daly, "Theory of Health Science," 151.

45. Byrne, "Evolutionary Science," is helpful on this topic.

materialism and dualism."⁴⁶ Daly's intention is to offer an alternative to what he calls the *hybrid* standard biomedical model. He cites GEM as "a unified method for investigating the natural and historical dimensions of the world in which we live and seek to thrive."⁴⁷ Daly also addresses the role of models in understanding the basis of health science and healthcare. He refers to Ian McWhinney's *Textbook of Family Medicine*. McWhinney, an early proponent of the patient-centered clinical method, advocated explicit attention to the philosophical foundations of medicine. Daly notes that McWhinney sets up "an interesting dynamic there between two ways of thinking about these foundations, one based on systems theory and the other on the traditional notion of a great chain of being"⁴⁸ to explain the biological basis of family medicine. With McKinney, Daly acknowledges

> The key role of George Engel's biopsychosocial (BPS) model in calling attention to the mutual interaction of a hierarchy of systems within and between individuals with respect to health and disease. On the other hand, the physical exchange of information that occurs between different systems levels, both individual and social, is not the same as what a patient actually feels in being well or ill or what occurs in the intersubjective communication of meaning between caregiver and patient.⁴⁹

As we saw, Daly distances himself from the BPS model. Daly calls attention to the mutual interaction of a hierarchy of systems within and between individuals with respect to health and disease. Nonetheless, I argue that his "GEM model" underestimates some key facets of Lonergan's achievement such as how he praised Robert Doran's work on primary and secondary process.⁵⁰ This undermines Daly's attempt to uphold GEM as an exemplary model for understanding and expounding what medical doctors do in their practice. His model is in my view *a one-phase* approach to Lonergan's work that neglects the two-phase (diphase) stressed in *MiT*. It minimizes the role of conversion in Lonergan's overall opus. Daly does allude in passing to "moral conversion," but does not go into all that is implied in such. True, Daly does stress the central role of the virtually unconditioned of judgment

---

46. Daly, "GEM Model," 421.
47. Daly, "GEM Model," 421.
48. Quoting Lovejoy, *Great Chain*.
49. Daly, "GEM Model," abstract, 421. Daly refers to Engel's model as seen in Evans et al., "Form of Causation," fig. 4.
50. In "Horizons and Transpositions," Lonergan refers to the importance of "Robert Doran's primary process and of the intermediate zone that lies between it and secondary process." See below in "The Fifth Functional Specialty" for a more detailed account.

as explained in *Insight*. Daly illustrates this when addressing the question as to whether a patient has bacterial meningitis:

> This is a question for judgment, according to Lonergan, which falls under the general form, "Is it so?" When the clinician is able to answer yes, she not only relates abstract formulation to concrete instances (explanatory to experiential conjugates), but also knows that this is 'what is wrong,' factually, objectively, ontologically, not just analytically or logically. It is more than arriving at 'classifications in which an individual becomes a class instance.' The clinician is able to do this by asking and answering all the questions relevant to the patient's problem. In this case, the clinician arrives at what Lonergan calls the "virtually unconditioned."[51]

While Daly's near total neglect of religious conversion is understandable in light of his appeal to medicine as such, his failing to address in more depth the way Lonergan has dealt with intellectual conversion calls for clarification.[52] In short, Daly's model fails to do full justice to Lonergan's legacy—this undermines his own praiseworthy project. His one-phase model should be supplemented by transposing to medicine the eight-step FS approach developed in *MiT*. I seek to "upgrade" Daly's "GEM Model" by reaching further into Lonergan's extraordinary but all-too-often underappreciated or misunderstood breakthroughs in his later works.

---

51. Daly, "Theory of Health," 147. In the case of meningococcal meningitis, there is a classical correlation between this type of bacteria and infection of the meninges. Actual cases of meningococcal meningitis vary in a non-systematic fashion, which statistical method addresses in terms of probability. What is the incidence of meningitis in a given population? How much time elapses between onset of symptoms of meningococcal meningitis and death? How often does this organism affect the meninges compared to the pericardium or the synovial membrane of a joint? How often is bacterial meningitis caused by meningococcus compared to other organisms in various populations? Classical method and statistical method are complementary. One deals with the systematic as abstract and with the non-systematic as occurring (*Insight*, 137; see index for the meaning of conjugates).

52. All of us need healing attained through intellectual, psychic, moral, and religious conversions. Lonergan helps us understand how human consciousness can transcend false faith-science dichotomies and to evaluate the roles of the unconscious and of technology in our lives, and even the residual tribal elements that may subtly influence us.

The Later Lonergan's Breakthroughs—an Indispensable GEM-FS Process Element

In *MiT* and later works, Lonergan extended his views on GEM into the possibilities his method has for furthering intra-and interdisciplinary "FS collaboration" as a *process* based on the way humans come to know and act in their lives. My attempt to "upgrade" Daly's GEM model is done with this in mind. I "piggy-back" on Daly's views so as to "translate" his model into a GEM-FS based interdisciplinary *process* approach. Demonstrating the relevance of a GEM-FS approach to interdisciplinary work is necessary not only in regards to Daly's efforts, but, on a broader scale, to help overcome the near-paralysis of present "Lonergan studies" which have not found a way to adequately *implement* Lonergan's hope that GEM-FS become a movement able to "heal-and-create" in the world.

As noted, Daly stresses the mutual interaction of a hierarchy of systems within and between individuals with respect to health and disease. My suggested GEM-FS alternative in handling such interactions appeals to psychic and evolutionary process and to Daly's own praiseworthy distancing himself from George Engel's BPS mode. *But* this "distancing" would very much benefit from the later Lonergan's GEM-FS approach. As noted, Daly focuses on McWhinney's argument which argues in part that

> Knowing the subjective (or mental) dimension of illness involves hermeneutical understanding concerning meaning, but knowing the objective (or physical) dimension of illness involves empirical science concerning sense data.... These represent distinct levels of being, each with its own level of knowing.[53]

This differentiation of levels of being "is qualitative in contradistinction to the quantitative stratification of the BPS hierarchy, which depends primarily on differences in size and number."[54] As to how the mental and the physical are related epistemologically, McWhinney and Lonergan agree in principle. The distinction between subjective and objective data is artificial because perception and interpretation always go together. In medicine, that means that to be a skilled observer one needs to be trained in interpretation. But McWhinney leaves open the question as to how the mental and physical are related ontologically. Daly perceptively adds that this last point relates to a problematic that George Khushf identifies in attempting to "rethink

---

53. Daly, "GEM Model," 2, quoting McWhinney, *Textbook*, 80.
54. Daly, "GEM Model," 2, quoting McWhinney, *Textbook*, 80.

the core model that informs medicine,"[55] which takes for granted a sharp divide between facts and values. Biomedical models of health and disease presume that "explanation traces a path downward" to the level of cell biology or genetics or neuroscience and that causation "proceeds upwards"[56] from these levels to determine the functional state of the whole organism or network. Although Engel's BPS model took explicit account of the role of top-down determination of lower-level functioning in his BPS model, he excluded value from playing a truly "scientific" role in such determinations. Daly adds that more recent and less hierarchical medical models based on genomic versions of systems biology, such as "P4 medicine" also mention a third level of being, the transcendental, concerning which knowing is "contemplative."[57] Daly agrees with McWhinney that this is difficult to express in words. With Daly, I seek in Lonergan's work on the nature of values a sounder, more universal scientific basis to include the necessity of planetary healing in an age of transformation.

Psychophysics and neuroscience seek to empirically demonstrate the mind-body unity by relating increases in bodily energy to corresponding increases in mental activity. Does conscious experience arise in a brain or does a brain develop in conscious experience? Lonergan, like Husserl, opted for the latter. His unified theory of consciousness can be compared with neuroscientific approaches which are rapidly gaining ground.[58] GEM-FS approaches brain-mind questions by asking how linguistic formulations are descriptive and explanatory in analogical ways. It relates the common sense of all cultures to how the sciences and philosophy relate things to one another in theoretical conjugates. Our conscious experience and normal thinking processes help us interrelate the sciences with ethics in daily life. Its openness to Eastern spirituality (Appendix D) helps GEM-FS become

---

55. George Khushf, "Health as Intra-systemic Integrity," 444–45, accepts the move to understand health as intra-systemic integrity, but argues that health science and clinical practice are both "irreducibly interpretive" and "value-laden . . . The rate-limiting steps in the long-awaited molecular revolution (in healthcare) may depend more on new social and cultural forms . . . (than)] on a new technology or on filling in the missing term in a network diagram." For Khushf, as for Lonergan, facts and values cannot be disentangled.

56. Khushf, "Health as Intra-systemic Integrity," 445.

57. Daly, "GEM Model," 3.

58. Early psychophysics concentrated on the sensory system—as did the early Freud. Lonergan went beyond mirror-neuron automata. Mark Morelli, "Unified Theory," studies Associationism, whose roots go back to Hobbes, Hume, and the phenomenologists. Associationism—the idea that mental processes operate by the association of one mental state with its successor states—holds that all mental processes are made up of discrete psychological elements and that their combinations are made up of sensations or simple feelings.

transcultural. It helps us mediate our sense of wonder, our dreams and hopes, our desires and ideals, allowing us to "feedback-transcend" ourselves in ways that avoid a neuroscientific epi-phenomenalist physicalism and a biological determinism. GEM-FS, an ongoing process method, can help us promote East-West dialogue based on mysticism, thus laying a deeper basis for foundational interchanges among cultures and religions.

Towards a GEM-FS-Process Approach to Medicine[59] in an Age of Transformation

Referring to an article by Hood and Flores on the emergence of proactive P4 medicine, Daly writes:

> Systems biology and the digital revolution are together transforming healthcare to a proactive P4 medicine that is predictive, preventive, personalized and participatory. Systems biology—holistic, global and integrative in approach—has given rise to systems medicine, a systems approach to health and disease. Systems medicine promises to (1) provide deep insights into disease mechanisms, (2) make blood a diagnostic window for viewing health and disease for the individual, (3) stratify complex diseases into their distinct subtypes for a impedance match against proper drugs, (4) provide new approaches to drug target discovery and (5) generate metrics for assessing wellness. P4 medicine, the clinical face of systems medicine, has two major objectives: to quantify wellness and to demystify disease. Patients and consumers will be a major driver in the realization of P4 medicine through their participation in medically oriented social networks directed at improving their own healthcare. P4 medicine has striking implications for society—including the ability to turn around the ever-escalating costs of healthcare. The challenge in bringing P4 medicine to patients and consumers is twofold: first, inventing the strategies and technologies that will enable P4 medicine and second, dealing with the impact of P4 medicine on society—including key ethical, social, legal, regulatory, and economic issues. Managing the societal problems will

---

59. Approaches to medical decision-making include case-based reasoning, simple single-layer neural network, and probabilistic neural network. Michel Foucault analyzed the processes involved in the history of medical decision-making in eighteenth century France. See Foucault, *Foucault Reader*.

pose ... significant challenges. Strategic partnerships of a variety of types will be necessary to bring P4 medicine to patients.[60]

Historical Background to *Insight*'s Cognitional Theory: Its Importance as a Template for Evaluating Daly's GEM Model

The four P's, including the personalized, participatory, holistic stress on medicine, can, I believe, provide a transition point between Daly's GEM model which underplays the role of conversion in Lonergan's work, and an overall GEM-FS process approach. The latter is a more encompassing interpretation of Lonergan's work. I argue that Daly's approach to GEM is a halfway, somewhat anemic measure which a FS approach to, e.g., P4 can help remedy. Before pursuing this in greater detail in Parts III and IV, I shall first briefly comment on Lonergan's GEM-FS process method. The method can help us better understand who we are and what we may have failed to do in life. It can help us *radically* correct what ails us. Using this method, I seek to apply humanity's searches for universal values in the uncertain times we live in.[61]

Our times call for bridge-building. Lonergan's method when correctly understood and applied enables us to build needed bridges, but this requires that we move beyond conventional modes of thinking. People living on a globalized planet, exposed to ideologies and traumatized by the results of pursuing self-interests, need self-giving persons focused on the common good and universal values.

As we shall see later, Lonergan's entire lifework was dedicated to clearing a path for such a need. Daly's suggested GEM-based method for medicine seems to have underestimated GEM-FS's key roles. That means that there is a need to develop, with Lonergan, a universal diphase method that can help us get inside ourselves so that we can work together both in a general manner and in such specialized fields as medicine. Daly implicitly uses GEM-FS's two phases when he refers, for example, to Flores and Hood's

---

60. Daly, "GEM Model," 9, referring to Hood and Flores, "Personal View on Systems Medicine."

61. In a way, we humans have gotten too smart for our own good; too many of us have sacrificed wisdom. Today's globalization, digitalization, and new technologies present us with rare challenges and opportunities. We live in a world of instant communication but we are not sufficiently aware of how our actions impact other human beings and the climate on which we depend for food, indeed for our very survival. Inequalities between rich and poor, as well as differences among religious fanatics, atheists, and secularists further exacerbate our divides.

bidirectional[62] flow of information model, but he does not draw GEM-FS's full implications to the detriment of his own overall aim. The "bidirectional" is somewhat in the line of the FS's eight specialties, a hint Daly does not pick up on. I shall argue that Lonergan's approach to collaborative networking provides not only a universal, practical-and-in-depth approach to values, but also a reliable "feedback-matrix tool" to do so. This twin ability can be extremely helpful, for example, in *the process of finding solutions* in the face of crises such as the COVID-19 pandemic.[63] It is with this goal in mind that Parts III and IV explore the roles of the eight FS in more depth. My present brief overview of Lonergan's books *Insight* and *Method in Theology*[64] is a preliminary introduction to this larger task.

Lonergan was influenced by many thinkers in such fields as mathematics, philosophy, theology, ethics, and the social sciences. Not the least of these influences was that of Edmund Husserl (1859–1938), a pioneer in science, mathematics and philosophy. Husserl was inspired by Franz Brentano (1838–1917) who himself had tried to adapt Aristotle's works to the modern world with particular emphasis on the Scholastic notion of intentionality. Husserl did not coin the term "phenomenology," but he is its father. Phenomenologists attempt to describe human experiences (and the "things themselves") without metaphysical and theoretical speculations. Husserl wrote about the intentionality of human consciousness. Linking our conscious intentional operations in all fields of human endeavors became one of the distinct marks of Lonergan's method.[65] Phenomenology,

62. According to Daly, in medical models such as Hood and Flores's P4 model, all levels or nodes of an organism's functioning are thought to be systematically and quantitatively related to one another via the bidirectional flow of information. According to these models, the emergent properties of whole systems differ from that of their parts, but the relations between whole and part, like the relations between parts, are to be understood in engineering or algorithmic terms. In contrast to these models, the GEM model of health distinguishes systematic and non-systematic relations both in world order (the way the universe is ordered) and in the way that living things like human beings are organized. See Daly, "GEM Model," Parts 1 and 2.

63. Bias prevents the dynamism of our minds from fully attending to experience, understanding and making impartial judgments despite the evidence. Group biases may explain why some disregard the evidence in the face of the COVID-19 pandemic influenced as they are by local community interests.

64. To broaden our perspective beyond the field of medicine, I appeal to universal values developed in the world religions and by philosophers and ethicists throughout the ages. First, I put *Insight* in a historical perspective so as to briefly answer the question as to why Lonergan criticized philosophers' not-seldom mistaken presuppositions.

65. In doing so, Lonergan took pains to correct some shortcomings in Husserl's views. He faulted phenomenology for being too focused on scientific description at the expense of a valid scientific explanation. This resulted in a phenomenological "abstract looking from which the looker and the looked-at have been dropped because of their

for example, can help us address a person's experience of illness so as to enable health care providers to enhance their understanding of it.

Lonergan helps us understand how inquiries in any field of study can be related to actual conditions of life. In *Insight*, he notes that description relates things to ourselves and to our senses while explanation relates things to one another within a universal viewpoint. Explanatory understanding demands the creation of a theoretical language based on the various differentiations of human consciousness. This basic distinction between description and explanation is central to all of Lonergan's analyses. In the natural sciences, explanatory understanding is made possible by mathematics. In the human sciences, mathematics plays a lesser role in relation to how humans actually understand and how they freely decide.[66]

In *MiT*, and some of his later works, Lonergan, like Paul Ricoeur, dwelled on human capabilities, but also on how we humans are vulnerable in so many aspects of our lives—in our thoughts, in our activities. Both saw persons as responsible for their actions. Both rejected claims "that the self is immediately transparent to itself or fully master of itself."[67] Lonergan refers to Ricoeur's notion of moral defect:

> Among the Hebrews, moral defect was first experienced as defilement, then conceived as the people's violation of its covenant with God, and finally felt as personal guilt before God, where, however, each later stage did not eliminate the earlier but took it over to correct it and to complement it.[68]

Self-knowledge presupposes one's relations with others in the various worlds or spheres of influence one is involved in. Lonergan closely examines the process of coming to self-knowledge in *Insight* and other works. As in my previous writings, I continue to closely align GEM with *MiT*'s FS. This means that I speak of Lonergan's overall method as being a "GEM-FS process"[69] that focuses on our four "knowing-doing" operations as studied

---

particularity and contingence"(*Insight*, 440). Nevertheless, phenomenology can be applied to the first-person experience of illness so as to illuminate this experience and enable health care providers to better understand it. If Husserl helped bridge Greek and scholastic philosophy with modern philosophy, Lonergan helps us bridge Husserl's abstract approach derived from mathematics with insights into how all humans, in fact, use their own conscious intentional operations in every aspect of their lives.

66. Lonergan, *Insight*, 316–21.
67. See Pellauer and Dauenhauer, "Paul Ricoeur," para. 2.
68. Lonergan, *MiT*, 88. Lonergan refers to Ricoeur, *Finitude et culpabilité*.
69. The idea that even religious truth is in "process" emanates from several divergent philosophical strands such as pragmatism, process philosophy, Marx, Blondel, etc. For the latter influence, see Baum, *Man Becoming*.

in *Insight*. A crucial point in so doing is to "interlink" these self-corrective, knowing-doing operations at work within the four levels of our cognitional patterns with the reduplicative aspects these assume within the eight FS as developed in *MiT* (as illustrated in Fig. 1) and developed in Parts II to IV. This means that Lonergan's thought can be and should be applied in interdisciplinary ways to life's realities.

A Basic Account of Lonergan's Cognitional Theory

Having briefly situated *Insight*'s historical genesis, I turn to give a basic account of Lonergan's cognitional theory so as to bring his original but challenging work a bit more "down to earth" as it were—an effort that stresses the later Lonergan's post-*Insight* publications.

Lonergan lists the following as the "basic pattern of operations": seeing, hearing, touching, smelling, tasting, inquiring, imagining, understanding, conceiving, formulating, reflecting, marshalling and weighing the evidence, judging, deliberating, evaluating, deciding, speaking, writing.[70] We are all familiar with these operations. Note that all of them are intentional—a potentially misleading term. Usually one thinks of "intentional" as being roughly synonymous with the adjective "deliberate." Lonergan does not imply that intentional operations are deliberate; rather, he refers to the fact that each of these operations requires an object. For example, one cannot see without seeing something, nor can one imagine without imagining something, and so on. The "something" in each case is what Lonergan calls the object. "To say that the operations intend objects is to refer to such facts as that by seeing there becomes present what is seen, by hearing there becomes present what is heard, by imagining there becomes present what is imagined, and so on, where in each case the presence in question is a psychological event.[71] Operations necessarily first imply an operator—that is, a subject who is conscious by way of his/her four intentional operations. Lonergan describes a subject's movement through the operations on the empirical, intellectual, rational, and responsible levels as being respectively that of experiencing, understanding, judging, and deciding. Second, our consciousness expands when, from mere experiencing, we turn to the effort to understand what we have experienced. Thirdly, in coming to know there emerges within the content of our acts of understanding the question as to whether one is merely dealing with a bright idea or whether one is really on to something. By judging is one endeavoring to settle what really is so?

---

70. Lonergan, *MiT*, 6.
71. Lonergan, *MiT*, 7.

Fourthly, when one judges that one has judged correctly as to the facts, one begins to deliberate on what we are to do about them.[72] Every act of knowing involves a pattern of experiencing, understanding, and judging. The fourth level, that of deciding, while extremely important, is not constitutive of knowing. We come to know many things without making any decision about what to do with them. The first three patterns in knowing may be summarized as follows:

1. Experiencing. If someone is in a deep coma, or is in a dreamless sleep, he/she cannot come to know anything. Experiencing is part of knowing. But, contrary to empiricist philosophers' claims, in itself it does not constitute knowledge. What we experience is, of itself alone, nothing more than scraps of data.

2. Understanding. To the data of our experience we put the question, "What is it?" (the "question for intelligence"). Answers come through insights. We have an insight whenever we come to understand something. Merely arriving at an insight does not constitute knowledge. In trying to understand, one may arrive at correct answers but also at incorrect ones.

3. Judging. With regard to an insight, one asks "Is it so?" This is the question for reflection. It is here that one judges whether there are adequate grounds to support one's initial insights. The question for reflection is answered with further "reflective" insights that should lead to correct judgments.

One can expand on these three cognitional operations by putting into context how Lonergan arrived at his cognitional theory. As explained in *Insight* and *MiT*,[73] GEM seeks to answer three basic questions:

1. "What am I doing when I am knowing?" (The cognitive, psychology-based question). For Lonergan, in order to know how we come to know anything, we need to pay close attention to what goes on in our consciousness. He invites each one to *empirically examine his/her consciousness and the mind's processes of knowing*. One observes how people actually operate when they formulate and verify ideas. Scientists consider data (the first step in knowing). The data are not divorced from how a mind operates as it asks questions so as arrive at answers. Cognitional theory identifies, distinguishes, and relates the sets of acts we perform whenever we know in mathematics, in the

72. Lonergan, *MiT*, 9.
73. Lonergan, *MiT*, 25.

natural and human sciences, as well as when we engage in every day commonsense living.

2. "Why is doing that knowing?" (The epistemological question). *Insight* argues that genuine human knowledge is based on one's personal self-appropriation and an affirmation of one's own rational self-consciousness. It invites readers to appropriate their own conscious operational acts of experiencing, understanding, judging, and deciding—in theology or any other discipline.

3. "What do I know when I am knowing?" (The metaphysical question that transposes Aquinas's cognitional theory into contemporary contexts). GEM-FS is a generalized, transformative process method that can help a person access his/her data of consciousness[74] and conscious intentional operations in ways that interact with other persons while correctly handling various kinds of data.

These three basic questions must be addressed in that order. Lonergan's GEM (a cognitional theory) is influenced by the method of inquiry as pursued in the sciences. So as to rethink the Cartesian *Cogito ergo sum* ("I think therefore I am") in *Insight*, chapter 11, Lonergan invites readers to affirm their own existence—not with a mere *cogito*, but through a judgment based on reflective insights. Later in *Insight*, Lonergan explores an epistemology and a metaphysics that reject the a priori presuppositions of Kant and Husserl. Like many modern philosophers, Lonergan disagrees with Leibniz and Christian Wolf who presumed that a rationalist metaphysics has priority over epistemology. He reverses formerly taken-for-granted hierarchies in such philosophies. He transforms the metaphysics of Aristotle and Aquinas by situating them (see Appendix A) within his GEM methodical context. His transposition of metaphysics means that a GEM metaphysics depends on a correct epistemology which in turn depends on a prior knowing of one's own knowing. Metaphysics, a transcendental integration of heuristic structures, thus depends on one's own self-knowledge. Only then can one ground, unify other knowledge.[75]

---

74. The way that Lonergan "unobtrusively" introduces the data of consciousness in his canon of selection in chapter 3 of *Insight*, 95, is noteworthy. He notes in the section, "The Restriction to Sensible Data," that in their "essential features" both the data of sense and consciousness have "sensible consequences." Just above that passage he speaks of "a trap for the unwary" as to grasping the full implications of an "appropriate division of labor." His aim here is to show how we can validly transpose private acts into a public domain—a key accomplishment of *Insight*.

75. Lonergan, *Insight*, 410–616.

Lonergan's Critical Realism Goes beyond Phenomenology

Lonergan refers to GEM as a critical realism—partially grounded in the Aristotelian-Thomist traditions. Humans can and do make true judgments of fact and of value. Lonergan's critical realism seeks to ground knowing and valuing in a way analogous to what Kant had attempted. But he avoids both Kant's and Husserl's notions of intuition. Lonergan considered intuition equivalent to "seeing" which is why he avoided it. Instead, he distinguished between inquiry and investigation. By investigation he means

> The process that is initiated in the subject by intellectual wonder or curiosity, that methodically seeks, accumulates, classifies possibly relevant data, that gradually through successive insights grows in understanding and so formulates hypotheses that are expanded by their logical presuppositions and implications to be tested by further observation and perhaps experiment.[76]

He stresses that within this process method there occur both inquiry and insights. Insights respond to inquiry which is the active principle that intends an unknown. While inquiry and insights occur within the larger process of learning, inquiry is "the dynamic principle that gradually assembles all the elements in the compound that is human knowing."[77] Intuition, on the other hand, short-circuits insight and judgment. GEM traces to their roots the sources of the meanings and values that constitute personality, social orders, and historical developments. GEM-FS systematically explores the ways such meanings and values are distorted. It proposes a framework for collaboration among disciplines to overcome basic philosophical distortions that negatively affect our lives. It aims to promote sound ways of living.[78]

---

76. Lonergan, "Theories of Inquiry," 34.

77. Lonergan, "Theories of Inquiry," 34.

78. People often attribute different meanings to words. This is due to the polymorphism of consciousness which Lonergan addresses in the chapter "The Method of Metaphysics," in *Insight*. On p. 449, he speaks, of the incubus of a fallacy which would have it that "to doubt mechanist determinism was to doubt the validity of the sciences." After touching on Einstein, quantum mechanics, etc., he writes on p. 451 that we face "the fundamental task in working out an appropriate technical language for philosophy" which would imply exploring "the range of meanings that may be assumed by the basic variables: knowledge, reality and objectivity." This leads him to speak on p. 452 of the polymorphism of consciousness, the one and only key to philosophy." This polymorphism is balanced with the isomorphic structure between knowing and known, of knowledge and expression, of mathematical with physics, *Insight*, 138, 339, 576. In *MiT*, 21, Lonergan simply says "that *one and the same process* constructs both elementary acts of knowing into a compound knowing and elementary objects of knowing into the

Insight analyzes the changes of mind involved in doing science. It draws out the implications of scientific performance. For Lonergan, an adequate analysis of science, far from justifying positivist or empiricist visions of scientific understanding, reveals the need of a critical realism that can coherently integrate all the sciences while addressing the question of God and grounding moral and religious concerns. The key to all this is a critical realism, an ability to change one's mind regarding mind itself.

As distinguished from Husserl's intentional phenomenology,[79] GEM is based on human awareness, not only of sensed experiences and feeling, but also of other mental acts such as imagining, inquiring, understanding, questioning, hypothesizing, formulating, marshalling evidence, judging and so on. GEM stands to the data of consciousness as the empirical method stands to the data of sense. Just as there are data about the material universe studied in the natural sciences, so there are also data about the working of the human mind. For Lonergan, the data of consciousness are as ascertainable as are the data of sense in the natural sciences. They are the starting point for one's knowing of knowing; they constitute its justification. Generalizing the notion of data to include the data of consciousness as well as those of sense is pivotal to an authentic GEM. It helps account for disciplines that deal with humans as constituting meaning and values. From the compound data of sense and of consciousness, one ascends through hypotheses to verification of the operations by which humans deal with what is meaningful and what is valuable: hence, GEM, is a *"generalized* empirical method"[80] that can be, and should be functionally *specialized* (GEM-FS) as Lonergan did in *MiT*.

Insight shows that genuine human knowledge is a personal self-appropriation of one's own rational self-consciousness. It invites readers to

---

compound object." Gerard Walmsley, *Philosophic Pluralism*, argues that the polymorphism of consciousness in *Insight* needs the further exploration of interiority given in *MiT*. Accordingly, I argue that Daly's use of GEM is also in need of GEM-FS interiority. Lonergan, *MiT*, 268, writes that conversion is only implicit in the first 3 FS; he adds: "While dialectic does reveal the polymorphism of consciousness—still it does no more: it does not take sides. It is the person who takes sides." Taking sides depends on whether one has been converted The need for conversion is central to Lonergan's work—that includes studying the deeper implications of the processes involved in intellectual, moral and religious conversions.

79. In his *Logical Investigations*, Husserl developed a view according to which conscious acts are primarily intentional, and a mental act is intentional only in case it has an act-quality and act-matter. Lonergan's overriding concern was with readers' developing an understanding of their own acts of understanding, which can then serve as a dynamic and invariant base for future personal and interpersonal development. He initially employed a form of phenomenological investigation that in later years he called "intentionality analysis."

80. Lonergan, *Insight*, 96.

appropriate t*heir own fourfold process of conscious intentional operations* of experiencing, understanding, judging, and deciding. It considers a very wide range of problems such as philosophy, mathematics, natural science (especially physics), ethics, psychoanalysis, literature, and theology. Coming to insights in any field has both distinctive and similar patterns. *Insight* helps a reader come to "understand understanding." It focuses on knowing's dynamic structure, on that structure's invariant patterns shared by all knowers in whatever discipline they might venture. Lonergan succinctly summarizes the process: "Thoroughly understand what it is to understand, and not only will you understand the broad lines of all there is to be understood but also you will possess a fixed base, an invariant pattern, opening upon all further developments of understanding."[81]

In his treatment of classical laws, Lonergan states that "verification is of formulations, and formulations state 1) the relations of things to our senses, and 2) the relations of things to one another."[82] It follows that formulations contain *experiential conjugates* (correlatives whose meaning appeals to the content of *human experience*) and pure or explanatory conjugates which are correlatives "defined implicitly by empirically established correlations, functions, laws, theories, systems."[83]

Some Important Implications of *Method in Theology*'s Eight FS and Its Two Phases

Lonergan's transcendental GEM recognizes all valid insights in scientific and philosophical methods but seeks to correct any shortcomings. Applying his method worked out in *Insight* to theology, *MiT* reviews the main procedures for engaging in theology and potentially in all other disciplines. After treating notions of the human good, meaning, and religion, *MiT* deploys Lonergan's discovery of eight functional specialties (FS) as applicable to theology, namely, research, interpretation, history, dialectic, foundations,[84] doctrines, systematics and communication. Since human consciousness is intentional, the interplays between our conscious intentional operations gives rise to *MiT*'s "diphase FS method," that is its division of the FS into two phases. The first four FS deal with theology as indirect discourse, whereby the theologian learns from the past (in the mediating phase); in the mediated

81. Lonergan, *Insight*, 22.
82. Lonergan, *Insight*, 102.
83. Lonergan, *Insight*, 102.
84. One might say that GEM is the "foundational touchstone" on which to apply the FS to any subject.

phase, the last four FS develop theology as a "direct discourse." This enables theologians to tackle contemporary and future problems. It was Lonergan's ability to show the critical importance of the data of consciousness and interrelating these data with the data of the senses in all human activities that made *Insight* distinctive. Two *Insight* breakthroughs are that it shows that 1) our intentional operations are conscious and 2) our data of consciousness are as valid and necessary in all human endeavors as are the data of sense. These two *Insight* breakthroughs help us personally appropriate our thought processes[85] leading to our possibly being converted intellectually, morally, religiously. They are also at the base of the mediating and mediated phases spelled out in *MiT*'s eight FS.[86] The eight FS mean that the transcendental precepts, "be attentive, be intelligent, be reasonable, be responsible"[87] (AIRR) can be, as suggested in Fig. 1, reduplicatively-reprised in inverse order in GEM-FS's second phase. This is what I will attempt to do in Parts II to IV below. Our dynamic AIRR transcendental imperatives dynamically "code," as it were, GEM's interlocking sets of terms and relations with our intellectual faculties providing "a higher integration of the psychic and the psychic providing a higher integration of the organic."[88] Each level involves its own laws terms and relations so that later in the text I speak of GEM-FS

85. Lonergan captures in theory what we actually do concretely when we think: he helps us appropriate our own thought processes (a matter of self-appropriation). This text pivots on Lonergan's eight functional specialties which are a transformational-unifying framework. The framework interrelates many fields such as the human and "hard" sciences, philosophy, ethics, religious studies, mathematics etc. It interrelates such fields by relating all of them to the processes of the human mind. It was through such interrelating that Lonergan was able to transform and unify seemingly different approaches to the sciences and other fields of studies. The reader will have to judge for herself or himself whether I have helpfully related Lonergan's transformative-unifying framework to the process of trying to upgrade Daly's GEM model.

86. Let us not forget that GEM-FS *has to be implemented*. I have gotten positive feedback on my attempts to apply Lonergan's method (GEM-FS) to climate-change strategies, to global community efforts, and to interfaith, interdisciplinary endeavors. It has now occurred to me that GEM-FS should really be a "GEM-FSI," that is a *generalized* empirical method functionally *specialized method to be implemented* through social justice, interfaith dialogue, etc. (This might involve GEM-FSI sub-strategies.) Without implementation, Lonerganians will continue to spin their wheels, but will not succeed in changing the world for the better as Lonergan hoped and urged. On Lonergan's economic manuscripts and their relevance to *Insight*, see Shute, "Two Fundamental Notions," and Shute, "Collaboration." Fig. 1 illustrates how GEM-FS *creates* from below upwards but is dependent on *healing processes* from above downwards. In *CWL* 15, 21 on economics, Lonergan stresses the importance of both the productive and exchange processes of goods and services.

87. Lonergan, *MiT*, 231.

88. Lonergan, *Insight*, 494.

conversions being an analogue to how mRNA works in our bodies to ward off threats.

Tad Dunne has illustrated the process as follows (without mentioning *MiT*'s mediating-mediated phases, nor the reduplicative feedback implied in the diagram):

Level of Transcendence	*Retrieving the Past*		*Moving into the Future*	
Being Responsible	↑	**Dialectic**	↓	**Foundations**
Being Reasonable	↑	**History**	↓	**Doctrines / Policies**
Being Intelligent	↑	**Interpretation**	↓	**Systematics / Plans**
Being Attentive	↑	**Research**	↓	**Communications / Implementations**

Fig. 1 implicitly correlates the data of sense and consciousness with the eight FS in ways that suggest *MiT*'s two phases underpinned by the reduplicative feedback process based on our knowing-doing operations as a formally dynamic, self-correcting process. Just as the circulatory system in animals and in humans transport nutrients, gases and waste through their respective systems, or just as the vascular system fulfills an analogous function in plants, or again as just as any political body is organized to govern, so Fig. 1 suggests how one might portray *MiT*'s mediating-creative and mediated-healing phases as proposed by Lonergan in *MiT*.

The bottom three rows of functions in Fig. 1 are familiar to anyone involved in practically any enterprise. The top row of functions is less familiar, but it represents Lonergan's clarification of the evaluative moments that occur in any collaboration for improving human living,[89] based as they are on a correct functioning of our four conscious-intentional levels of cognitional operations. It is from this fact that Lonergan developed in *MiT* two mediating-mediated phases which involve a reduplicative feedback process[90] based on human operations, a process that can be applied in cooperative ways. GEM-FS process depends on the successive levels illustrated in the left column of Fig. 1. These four levels correspond to the four transcendental precepts, be attentive, be intelligent, be reasonable, be responsible (AIRR) that Lonergan often invokes.

An important point which I pursue in Parts II to IV is that for GEM-FS, operating implies both cooperating and interdisciplinary collaboration—not only among individuals but among organized, social entities. Cooperation is based on the operations; collaboration is at the heart of *MiT*'s eight functional specialties. Fig. 1 illustrates the pivotal roles of our operations which inform and are reduplicatively transposed in eight FS. The reduplicative feedback process illustrated in Fig. 1 is also applicable to processes involving judgments of value. People in various cultures do perceive values differently; they make judgments of value partially based on their different perceptions. Some people are attracted to sensible things, others less so. It can be a problem for us to respond appropriately to one's own feelings or those of others. Often, we misunderstand what is at stake in certain situations or we remain indifferent to what does not concern us directly—though war and violence anywhere wreak havoc. The arrows in Fig. 1 show that there is a going back and forth between knowing-doing operations when a person or a group sort out different scenarios in a given situation. Deciding on courses of action is a process not restricted to individuals. Small and large groups—even the politics guiding nations are constantly engaged in such processes. The important point is that the same basic process informs the knowing-doing operations of individuals or of large entities. Fig. 1 draws out some implications of the relation between how our minds operate, and

---

89. Dunne, "Bernard Lonergan." My own interpretation of "reduplicative feedback" can be a key to link GEM-FS implementation. Fig. 1 implies that the FS are designed for communities of scholars and scientists using the feedback processes of their own operations. My text assumes that one's work can be tested by others. Implied in this testing process is Lonergan's differentiations of consciousness translated into communal contexts. A key point of this text is highlighting the move from dialectic to foundations, from the mediating-creative phase to the mediated-healing phase so as to help bolster Daly's arguments.

90. I stress the importance of process as an unifying dynamic function at the heart of GEM-FS; it is this dynamic function-capability that sets Lonergan's work apart from that of others. I seek to integrate these in ways that serve as a basis for interdisciplinary, interreligious cooperation as outlined in Parts II and III.

how the FS operate—both involve a reduplicative feedback process. Fig. 1 helps explain my efforts to draw out the implications of such feedback processes in GEM-FS—the central theme of this book. Just as Lonergan insisted that the active process of knowing goes beyond perception (a fact that we cannot deny if we are to understand Lonergan's lifework), so ideally his eightfold FS process method should be implemented[91]—not get short-circuited—if we are to transform societies for the better and conduct viable, helpful interfaith dialogues. (See Appendix D.) I argue that the FS, are, in effect, an integrated-integrating process method for cross-fertilizing the sciences and humanities with needed pertinent ethical and religious values. Processes of judging and deciding can get horrendously complicated, as is, for example, the case in assessing and delivering on global health needs. But at bottom, the process of coming to decisions and acting on them functions in analogical ways in both personal and group decisions. It is an important GEM-FS breakthrough that the FS are based on this analogically similar mode of knowing-doing operations in all human activities. In any case, the process must not be short-circuited.

MiT focuses mainly on the discipline of theology. I argue that "a reduplicative feedback" process exists between how 1) our knowing-doing operations work in our daily lives and 2) how these operations work in and inform the entire functional specialization process. In the latter case, there may arise a complicated process of going back and forth in each specialty, and in the entire reduplicative process of linking the specialties within one particular field of study or across all disciplines. Fig. 1 suggests how the FS might help ground judgments of value[92] to underpin modern society's efforts to tackle its problems by recognizing and living according to authentic values. I turn to very briefly outline ways specialists in various fields can and should collaborate using the transformative process method outlined in *MiT*'s two mediating-mediated phases.[93]

---

91. The analogies and even reinforcements between doing theology and/or any academic or scientific work need to be operative in the eight reduplicative, complementary specialized uses of our intentional cognitional operations. This requires implementation. Foundations is the key FS for such implementation. If that key is missing, then all is for naught—the other specialties cannot effectively operate in self-transcendent ways. The groundwork has to be carefully laid. This book is an effort towards such, one that would help further reflection on how to collaborate across disciplines in our confuse, globalized world. Lonergan has given us many insights into how we can collaborate.

92. Lonergan's "Healing and Creating" stresses the biases and blind religious hatred that hinder human "creating." In the second healing phase the role of grace is clearly invoked in Lonergan's response to B. F. Skinner and Karl Marx.

93. McShane, "Heart," 64, writes that in early 1953, when Lonergan's superiors sent him to Rome to teach theology, he remarked in a letter, "I must try to finish and arrange

THE FIRST MEDIATING-CREATIVE PHASE

In the mediating phase, the first level of experience is correlated with research (FS 1). The second level of understanding is correlated with interpretation (FS 2). Here one is called to understand texts, authors, various movements, and oneself. The third level of judging is correlated with the study of the nature of history and of the historical horizons of various historians (FS 3). The fourth level of deciding involves one in dialectic. Dialectic explores how one exercises one's freedom in the various possible conversions (FS 4). This first mediating phase, which mainly focuses on the past, is followed by the mediated phase concerned with the present and the future. Another principle for the division between the two phases "is derived from the fact that our conscious and intentional operations occur on four distinct levels and that each level has its own proper achievement and end."[94] The interface of the two phases, outlined in Fig. 1, is at the heart, at the center of Lonergan's overall contribution to philosophy and to human studies, involving as it does a reduplicative feedback process.

THE SECOND MEDIATED-HEALING PHASE[95]

In the mediated-healing phase, beginning with the fourth level of deciding (FS 5), one makes a personal commitment, one becomes the foundational reality due to personal conversions. In FS 6, the third level of judging asks what policies may best implement universal values in our day. It asks for personal and group commitments. In FS 7, the second level of understanding deals with systematic shortcomings in care for life and the planet. In FS 8, one returns to the first level of experience through communications (with persons and communities). Returning to the level of experience enables one to address actual issues in life in general, in medicine and in other areas. Unless we fully engage in the second mediated-healing phase, GEM-FS is

---

for the publication of a first part of my work before my departure. It would be entitled, *Insight*, and the remainder could be named Faith, or Insight and Faith. The effect of this imposed move to Rome left those final chapters of *Insight* as massively compressed achievements. One effect, however, must be noted: the non-inclusion in *Insight* of considerations of personal relations is a feature of its concrete theological context." Lonergan remedied this anomaly by writing *MiT* in the 1960s. It may be that Daly has underestimated this fact in devising his GEM model that seems to underestimate the crucial role of FS 5–8 in *MiT*.

94. Lonergan, *MiT*, 133.

95. The first phase arises from a multiplicity of data, the second "descends from the unity of a grounding horizon towards the almost endlessly varied sensibilities ... and tastes of mankind" (Lonergan, *MiT*, 142).

distorted—unhinged from its potential of constructively dealing with constant changes.

How *MiT*'s Diphase Eight FS Open Up New Horizons in Fields Such as Medicine[96]

We might say that GEM-FS can be called a "Living GEM" due to its being diphase and to its emphasis on *mediated* foundations. Such a living GEM is constantly adaptable. This feature may be particularly important in medicine. Daly's single-phase approach to GEM underplays the diphase GEM-FS approach Lonergan developed in *MiT*. The challenge is to transpose Daly's effort into a diphase process method more faithful to Lonergan's overall legacy. Matthew Lamb, for example has provided sound foundations to adapt Lonergan's work to life's actual realities. Lamb stresses praxis—not as a technique—but as helping facilitate socially transformative action.[97] I follow Lamb's praxis-oriented approach in adjusting Daly's insufficiently functionally-adaptable approach.

In *MiT*, Lonergan does follow tradition in his approach to theology, but he takes a functional perspective in doing so. He conceives theology as mediating "between a cultural matrix and the significance and the role of a religion in that matrix."[98] This original notion of theology means that it is not identified with a religion. Rather, Lonergan conceives theology functionally. It should help a religion communicate with a culture. This means that one does theology in ways relevant to a culture—in ways that differ from classical theologies. For a classicist, both culture and theology are conceived statically; theology is modeled on views of science and culture as permanently valid: one reflects upon an object's nature. Lonergan is not concerned with the nature of theology. Rather, his empirical notion of culture leads him to reflect on theology's method. That means that, like

---

96. One may ask to what extent can one understand and "live by" the eight FS of *MiT* if one has not read or understood in full depth the self-discovery process of knowing developed in *Insight*? Matthews' *Lonergan's Quest* is restricted to a study of *Insight*. Such a restriction may "excuse" Daly for focusing mostly on *Insight*'s treatment of the four levels of knowing-doing while neglecting *MiT*'s second phase.

97. Lamb's *Solidarity*, is concerned with "eternal values." It proposes a fivefold typology that embodies the eternal and necessary structures of reality. To counter the claims of contemporary secular culture as to ethics, Lamb stresses praxis—not as a technique—but as helping facilitate socially transformative action. In this spirit, one can use GEM-FS as a common medium with a potentially universal application for effecting needed societal transformations. Praxis in this sense is equivalent to my GEM-FS process approach.

98. Lonergan, *MiT*, xi.

science and culture, theology can be thought of as ongoing and as cumulative. Lonergan wrote *Insight* to prepare himself for what eventually became *MiT*. He wanted to develop his theological method based on the normal intellectual operations of theologians so as to make explicit how these conscious, intentional operations function when one does theology.[99] *MiT* thus implements for theology the inherent drive normal persons have to be attentive, intelligent, reasonable, responsible (AIRR). Some would add "be in love" to AIRR so as to help ensure a certain continuity in theology. The drive towards authenticity[100] leads one to exclude mistaken "counter-positions" and to search for truth.

The normative or universal nature of human intentionality (as studied by Lonergan) results in a wedding of both continuity and renewal in theology. For example, genuine continuity is achieved in systematics when theologians realize that people of different times and places operate with the same normative structure of their conscious intentional operations. One thus seeks for continuity not in concepts, but in the common cognitional operations possessed by people of different times and places. One discovers that intentional consciousness seeks to build upon past achievements. While this implies development, it also means that contemporary work is linked to and continuous with the past.[101] *MiT* embodies Lonergan's methodological GEM-FS achievement; it stresses that it is human minds that do theology. Lonergan intended his theological method to be a specific application of the general transcendental method or intentionality analysis developed in *Insight*. *MiT* helps his readers discover the dynamic structure[102] of their

---

99. See *Second Collection*, 52, 268. GEM-FS—centered on eight interdependent functional specialties—can be applied to the humanities and sciences. It can provide an ethical bridge for human renewal for it uses humans' four basic operations' feedback character. The main potential of the eight FS is their enabling interdisciplinary cooperation. Such a cooperation, made possible by the reduplicative feedback pattern inbuilt within our basic operations' four conscious, intentional levels gives rise to a self-corrective process of knowing-doing. This reduplicative process is at the heart of Lonergan's method. The method can enable human cooperation in all fields and help find commonalities among thinking, intelligent persons of various backgrounds. This is because the eight FS place the humanities and the sciences within a common ground open to a universal application. The self-corrective nature of GEM-FS process is like a pearl hidden within intelligent persons' makeup—but potentially retrievable so as to be shared for the good of all.

100. On the other hand, "inauthenticity is realized by any single act of inattention, obtuseness, unreasonableness, irresponsibility" (Lonergan, "Dialectic of Authority," 7).

101. Lonergan, *MiT*, 326–27, 351–52.

102. One should stress the "process nature" of this dynamic structure which brings us in contact with what Lonergan calls the "paradoxical category of the "known unknown" that leads into *Insight*'s chapter on "Metaphysics as Dialectic" (Lonergan,

own conscious intentional operations. In *MiT*, he assumes his readers are cognitive, moral, and affective beings when they do theology. It is crucial to realize that Lonergan's theological method is in fact a method, not another resource for theological content, nor a solution of particular problems.[103] By making explicit the conscious, intentional operations of theologians, Lonergan wants to add clarity, intelligibility and precision to the theologian's task. He does so by outlining what human authenticity is in relation to theological activity. *MiT* appeals to, is based on such authenticity; it evaluates the degree to which a theologian operates in authentic human fashion. The word "operates" is crucial because Lonergan spent his life studying how our minds operate. Lonergan defines method as a "normative pattern of recurrent and related operations yielding cumulative and progressive results."[104] He adds that one has a method when there are distinct operations; each operation is related to the other; the relation forms a pattern; the pattern is verified as the correct way of performing the task; the pattern's operations may be repeated indefinitely and the results of such repetition are cumulative and progressive.[105]

Lonergan explains that putting method into theology means conceiving it as "a set of related and recurrent operations cumulatively advancing towards an ideal goal." He in no way wants to impose his method upon readers as if it were a procedure deduced from supposed first principles of theology. On the contrary, his method explores the set of operations that can help one do theology authentically. Lonergan does not expect his readers to unintelligently follow a set of prescribed steps (operations). He does invite them to attend to their own conscious activities and to find within themselves the relevant intentional conscious operations he describes. A reader will have to discover in his/her one's own experience the dynamic relationships leading from one operation to the next. This is in a nutshell the long process of self-appropriation outlined in *Insight*. Applied in *MiT*-fashion, this self-corrective process of learning can help one pursue an authentic theology—one relevant today. Were a reader to fail to properly

---

Insight, 555). There he explores being as the objective of the pure desire to know. Paradoxically, "we know of an unknown through our unanswered questions," and through the "higher integrations on the organic, psychic intellectual levels" which are "not static but dynamic systems. . . on the move" (Lonergan, *Insight*, 555).

103. Lonergan, *MiT*, xii, 24, 254.

104. Lonergan, *MiT*, 4.

105. Lonergan's four methods (classical, statistical, genetic, and dialectical) help us understand and answer many questions such as "how does the universe of being unfold?" See Lonergan, *Insight*, 509, 603; Lonergan, *MIT*, 287. See also Bigirimana, *Patterns*, which relates Lonergan's work to systems and information theory.

understand Lonergan's invitation to self-appropriation of one's own conscious activities, one would find his reflections on method "about as illuminating as a blind man finds a lecture on color."[106] For Lonergan, method is not a prescribed set of operations that can be blindly followed. "Neither discovery nor synthesis is at the beck and call of any set of rules."[107] Method is not a set of rules to be followed by a dolt, rather it is a framework of collaborative creativity; it is cumulative and progressive. Lonergan's invitation to be authentically creative also helps bring theology in line with, and tuned to the standards of modern science. Lonergan never rejects logic. He simply places logic within the wider context of method. He does include logic in his account of human intentional operations. Lonergan's method is not dictated merely by the objects of its investigations. Rather, his method is concerned with a subject's conscious intentional operations. Viewed in transcendental terms, it has a heuristic function, that is, it is an open structure for various types of inquiries.[108] In sum, *MiT* is not bound to deductive logic. Lonergan proposes a theology based on recurrent sets of operations which generate a GEM-FS process of theological activity progressively using more data and yielding ever more results. Research in FS 1 uncovers new data, provides new observations, possibly generating new insights that may verify or challenge a given hypothesis: "The wheel of method not only turns, but also rolls along. The field of observed data keeps broadening. New discoveries are added to old. New hypotheses and theories express not only the new insights but also all that was valid in the old."[109] Method's cumulative character engenders the conviction that, however, remote one may be from a complete explanation of all phenomena, at least it helps us be nearer to such an explanation "than we were."[110] In this text, I adapt Lonergan's GEM-FS principles to the field of medicine and its many specialties by "piggy-backing" on Daly's GEM model; I do so by insisting on *MiT*'s two phases.[111]

106. Lonergan, *MiT*, 7.
107. Lonergan, *MiT*, 6.
108. Lonergan, *MiT*, 6–7, 72, 85, 305.
109. Lonergan, *MiT*, 5.
110. Lonergan, *MiT*, 5.
111. In "Method in Action," note 49, Daly quotes Fred Crowe's "An Expansion" that touches on "decision and patterns of experience" from *MiT* onward when Lonergan speaks with increasing frequency about development from "above in terms of socialization, acculturation, and education." Daly comments: "As Crowe says, the operator of development from above is not just the individual subject, but more importantly subjects acting upon one another as subjects in personal relations." Along these lines, evolutionary theorists note that the first year of human life amounts to an extended period of social gestation unique among mammals in that it takes that long for human infants to reach the same stage of biological development that other mammals reach at

Rationale for Treating *Method in Theology*'s Eight FS within Two Phases

I have stressed *MiT*'s division into two phases whereby the mediating-creative phase treats the first four operational FS: research, interpretation, history, and dialectic. The second mediated-healing phase then treats the remaining four FS: foundations, doctrines, systematic, communications. Briefly said: 1) in *MiT*, Lonergan developed his method so as to implement GEM-FS' global bridging potential;[112] 2) this means that his method can be applied to other fields such as healthcare. Daly is, commendably, a pioneer in this regard. Yet, I also stress that Lonergan argues that contemporary theology has become specialized to the point that it can no longer be *one set* of operations; rather, it is *a series of interdependent sets* of operations. We can better appreciate this point by alluding to Lonergan's outline of three distinct forms of specialization.

1. Field specialization divides and subdivides the field of data so that one narrows the field of data with which one is concerned. It stresses the mediating phase.

2. "Subject" or "Department" specialization arranges and divides the results of its investigations. It stresses the mediated phase, but oversimplifies the mediating phase.

3. Lonergan's functional specialization method divides neither data nor results; rather it "distinguishes and separates *successive stages in the process from data to results*.[113] The FS give full attention to both mediating-mediated phases, showing their dynamic interdependence. Within each of GEM's two phases and between them, there occurs an interdependent complementarity as among the four levels of consciousness—since these levels determine the four specialties in each phase. An advantage[114] of

---

birth (Eldredge, 181–83). Even as adults, most of our decisions are determined not by immanently generated knowledge, but by socially patterned beliefs.

112. Because of its similarities to biological and artificial neural networks, neuromorphic computing is often described as the bridge between traditional computer processors and the relative strengths and weaknesses of the human brain. Neuromorphic computing, first developed by Carver Mead in the late 1980s, describes the use of very-large-scale integration systems containing electronic analog circuits to mimic neurobiological architectures present in the nervous system. See "Neuromorphic Computing."

113. Lonergan, *MiT*, 125–26.

114. By integrating the data of consciousness and of sense, GEM tackles many thinkers' biases towards foundations. Lonergan integrates the data of sense and consciousness as a way to engage in the FS. Humans must specialize; the FS enable us to cooperate in ways that can verify and extend human knowledge. Criticizing field and

functional specialization is the possibility of separate treatment of issues that "otherwise become enormously complex."[115]

Lonergan's Grasp of Historical Developments; the Need for Personal Commitments

In *Insight*, Lonergan analyzes changes of mind involved in doing science and draws some implications. He studies understanding so as to move from inadequate views on knowing, objectivity and reality to a full appreciation of the world of theory. In doing so, he explains how our minds attain valid knowledge. *Insight* radically revises notions of "already-out-there-now" interpretations of reality so prevalent among scientists and even among many philosophers. To arrive at genuine theories that do explain the real world means that one strives to know, not by merely imagining, but through thorough forms of understanding and tested judgments.[116] To a large extent, Lonergan based his GEM-FS analyses on the procedures in the modern empirical sciences. His writings show that he fully appreciated scientists' remarkable discoveries. Yet, he never naively acquiesced in what scientists say about science. His critical realism is rooted not just in experience, but in his analyses of understanding and types of judgments, as well as on roles of faith and love in our lives. He nuanced his critical realism by invoking the power of faith and love linking individual persons within communities. Medical doctors vary as to their personal beliefs and religious commitments, but GEM-FS accommodates all tenable positions. Faith sees God's glory reflected in a humanity fully alive and striving to make our world a better place for ourselves and for our children. To say that God created the world for his glory is to say that he created it "not for his own sake but for ours."[117]

---

data modes of specialization, Lonergan shows how functional specialization, based on our knowing-doing operations, can arrive at knowledge so as to act ethically. Daly's "Possibility" is a very insightful article that he should have explored further.

115. Lonergan, *MiT*, 153.

116. One arrives at the real through intelligent process that spontaneously moves through questioning, having insights/understanding, reflective understanding with our inborn self-corrective process at work, and finally with a judgment qualified to assert the reality of one's assertion.

117. Liddy, *Transforming Light*, 17. GEM-FS places us in the midst of things, *in medias res*. FS 4 and 5 are the key to transform existing but deficient modes of operation in life, including medical settings. From a Christian perspective, one might stress the roles of the cardinal and theological virtues which enable us to be more than passive spectators. GEM-FS maintains the constants of our conscious intentionality within endless diversity and applies them within a Lonergan-inspired worldview with its horizon

Lonergan's method has to be implemented. The question is how best to do this in interdisciplinary, ethical ways that also speak to the world religions and secularist minds? One's work needs to be tested by others; the FS provide a superb map for that need—thus enabling one to revise. That is the nub of the move from dialectic to foundations. I argue that that GEM-FS (as conceived for theology in *MiT*) can also be applied to all interdisciplinary work.[118]

Among some of the indispensable tools that Lonergan offers us to address human problems are his "healing-creating vectors."[119] I rely on these healing-creating endeavors to further develop Daly's model. If one were to identify a transformative "star" for rallying efforts to do this, one might say that it is judgments of value made from the heart and based on an "eye of love." Such an eye of love is needed to help resolve some of the conflicting issues on ways to provide needed health care to all. To do this, one may safely say that Lonergan left us not only a "GEM model" but that he transposed that model into a transformative GEM-FS-process approach whereby communities of inquirers can effectively coordinate and organize their efforts locally and globally. I develop such a process approach,[120] taking into account some of the many cultural and other realities affecting medicine today. Part II will briefly examine how the eight FS can be applied to medicine as well as other important areas. After an examination, in Part III, of the role of the first mediating-creative phase of *Method in Theology*, Part IV will stress the role of the conversions in *MiT*'s mediated-healing phase. The conversions provide both the linchpin and the transition points for a reduplicative-feedback process approach to medicine—a process that can be analogically applied to other fields.[121]

---

shifts, transformational ability, etc.

118. I follow Karl Rahner's view expressed in "Neue Ansprüche," 617–38, that *MiT* is a method that can be applied to fields other than theology.

119. Lonergan, "Healing and Creating," 100–109.

120. On the complementarity between Lonergan's *Insight* and his *MiT*, see Tracy, "Lonergan's Option."

121. In "Essays in Systematic Theology for a World Theology," Doran suggests adding a "ninth functional specialization" to Lonergan's version of eight. Doran would remove "the objectification of the normative subject" from FS 5, foundations, reducing it to a category. He claims his suggested category of "Horizons" would be an adequate way to mediate between the first and second phases of theology. Needless to say, my whole argumentation is contrary to Doran's proposal. See, for example, my arguments in the section "Transitional Issues" on expanding GEM-FS beyond the field of theology; see also Appendix D.

II

A Brief Overview of the Eight FS and of a GEM-FS Approach to Medicine[1]

Lonergan's FS are not disparate operations; they are successive stages of a united process of which they form a part. The eight FS involve many types of operations dynamically, intrinsically, and functionally related to one another. Each FS needs the others. Later FS presuppose and complement the earlier ones. This book is concerned with the strategies and policies that might apply Lonergan's method to medicine in ways that transpose and complement Daly's use of Lonergan's book *Insight*. I argue that by neglecting the diphase nature of GEM (including the implications of the mediated phase which touches on a person's personal decisions and actions as a result of the conversions), Daly undermines the deeper foundations of his own valid arguments. It is with this in mind that in Part II, I briefly examine the eight FS with a view to apply them in more detail to Daly's thesis in Parts III and IV. To put this in perspective, I started writing in March 2020 when the COVID-19 pandemic began to disrupt all normal ways of living for most humans. Medical doctors and specialized labs were still searching for types of vaccination against the virus—some of which have by now been

---

1. One may compare the moral problems of overcoming human biases to devising defenses against viruses.

approved. Background information on the structure and functions of virus genomes has been essential to this process.[2]

As just noted, Part II radically curtails all eight FS and their interrelationships. Suffice it to say at this point that FS 1 can be that of textual criticism which determines what is written. In this book, FS 1 is concerned with the data of health care. FS 2 takes over from FS 1 by interpreting the data on medicine and healthcare within the larger perspective of evolution and medical discoveries. FS 3, history, builds on interpretations; it seeks to construct a unified view point from accumulated texts—or data. An important point is that Lonergan's FS are not disparate functional operations; they are successive stages of a united process of which they form a part. The eight FS involve many types of operations dynamically, intrinsically, and functionally related to one another. Each FS remains incomplete without the others. Later FS's presuppose and complement the earlier ones. With this in mind, I shall now briefly touch on the final five FS which I shall develop in more detail when giving a fuller account of the eight FS in Parts III and IV; here, one must keep in mind the negative influence of human biases analyzed in Appendix B.

FS 4, *Dialectic*. If history judges upon what was going forward within a religion and its world, we also find that history reveals multiplicities of movements. Such movements are dynamic, concrete, and often contradictory. They call for responsibly deciding about the respective values of the various movements. Contradictions among particular movements provide the materials for the fourth FS, dialectic. Lonergan dryly notes that dialectic takes material from the conflicts between historical accounts of movements and "their conflicting theological interpretations."[3] Dialectic seeks a comprehensive viewpoint of different conflicts. This can be attained by understanding the relations and oppositions involved in contradictory historical movements. By critically comparing conflicts, dialectic seeks to clarify which given differences are irreducible, but it also strives to identify positions shared by opponents so as to better reconcile these. It stresses that conflicts may be seen as stages in a united process of development. Dialectic corresponds to the transcendental precept, "be responsible." Based on such an approach, dialectic decides which movements are coherently worthwhile and which need to take a more coherent position against biases. It adds to history by evaluating achievements and by discerning within them possible good or evil; it aims to purge viewpoints based on unsound reasons, mere

---

2. In previous publications I have proposed that GEM-FS can be considered as a "spiritual genome" that parallels in some ways the structures and workings of our physical genome.

3. Lonergan, *MiT*, 129.

ad hoc "explanations," on suspicions or even malice. It would do this by helping resolve conflicts—not by adding new data—but by finding a sounder, transformational horizon. In short, dialectic's function is to provide a comprehensive viewpoint which acknowledges meaningful, as opposed to mere contingent differences. It determines the grounds for such differences and seeks to eliminate unnecessary conflicts. Here the role of constitutive meaning is essential:

> It is in the field where meaning is constitutive that man's freedom reaches its highest point. There too his responsibility is greatest. There occurs the emergence of the existential subject, finding out for himself that he has to decide for himself what he is to make of himself. It is there that individuals become alienated from community, that communities split into factions, that cultures flower and decline, that historical causality exerts its sway.[4]

FS 5, *Foundations*. "Foundations objectifies conversion. They bring to light the opposite poles of a conflict in personal history."[5] Conversion, "a transformation of the subject and his world,"[6] changes a person's mind and heart: one's life takes on a new direction with new values, new concerns and new interests. Normally, it is an ongoing, lasting process, best discerned on the basis of its pivotal moments of judging and deciding. Foundations objectifies what flows from a person's depths—be it of an average person or of a learned ethicist, social critic, or theologian. Conversion, as an attunement of one's viewpoints that consciously reaches new decisions, opens one to a new horizon. Within such a new horizon, one will judge and evaluate one's world in new more meaningful, value-laden ways. In the case of a theologian, one's conversion will ultimately determine the teachings she/he finds meaningful or not meaningful. For Lonergan, a person operates knowingly, morally, and lovingly, in an ongoing process of being liberated from false horizons so as to reach a self-transcendent horizon blessed with truth, values, and goodness. Conversion is an existential, very personal occurrence. But Lonergan holds that it can be shared with persons and communities—yielding new horizons.[7] A community forms when its members hold in common a new horizon affecting that community's conscious operations. Such conversions deepen a community's understanding, direct its judgments, and influence its decisions. When speaking of such conversions—making these the object

---

4. Lonergan, "Dimensions of Meaning," 235.
5. Lonergan, *MiT*, 144.
6. Lonergan, *MiT*, 130.
7. Lonergan, *MiT*, 130.

of deliberation—one is operating within FS 5, foundations.[8] Foundations is the theological function pivoting on responsible decisions about what is valuable and meaningful and what is not. It is this fifth FS which defines the horizons within which a religion's beliefs can be evaluated. For Lonergan, in theology one establishes and distinguishes in FS 5 the horizons within which religious teachings have meaning. In our case, we shall consider and evaluate the decision-making horizons which enable or impede the needed decisions that have to be made when communities of various sizes, be they political or medical entities, address change.

FS 6, *Doctrines*. While *MiT*'s FS 6 is concerned with "doctrines," this book addresses FS 6 in terms of the policies needed to implement universal values in the light of the approaches to decision-making explained in FS 4 and FS 5. In FS 6, one concretizes ways whereby the transcendental precept, "be reasonable," is to be handled, in our case in devising policies in medicine. Lonergan argues[9] that in theology doctrines express judgments of fact and judgments of value. His notion of doctrines does not rest on arbitrary truths given immutably in divine revelation; rather it envisages doctrines as resulting from a definite process, and a determinate method. FS 4, dialectic, manifests the various options between attained truths and troubling errors of the past. FS 5, foundations, decides between truth and error by considering the options dialectic has uncovered. Doctrines stand within the horizon of foundations, without which they would lack meaning; they are judgments within a determinate horizon from which are selected and affirmed certain of the options presented in dialectic. Such judgments are compatible with and are intelligible within the foundational horizons of one's life and profession.

FS 7, *Systematics*. Lonergan notes that doctrines are not theology's terminal operation. This is because the facts and values affirmed in doctrines give rise to questions of meaning.[10] Systematics seeks to clarify what doctrines actually mean—and why this is so. It investigates how doctrines are conceptualized so as to resolve inconsistencies.[11] It corresponds to the transcendental precept, "be intelligent." As to this book's focus on medicine, FS7 can help us—after having understood relevant ongoing adaptations in medicine—evaluate the scenarios guiding the policies of persons, firms and nations in this area so as to reinforce Daly's "GEM model." That is to say, in the present case, the policy aspects of medicine are a key element.

8. Lonergan, *MiT*, 131.
9. Lonergan, *MiT*, 132, 299.
10. Lonergan, *MiT*, 336.
11. Lonergan, *MiT*, 132.

FS 8, *Communications*. Finally, as the result of the ongoing theological process, Lonergan clarifies this last FS (in which the other seven FS come to fruition and maturity) as that of mediating the results of theology to the "outside" community. Communications "is concerned with theology in its external relations."[12] Those relations may be with people involved in the arts, sciences, or with other religions. Communications can also be concerned with the relations that come from the transpositions that theology must make so that a religion can retain its integrity, while simultaneously appealing to the minds and hearts of many people. Such communication to different people means that the theologian must find common meaning and common understanding with those in one's audience. It is on that basis of common understanding that one can transmit one's acquired knowledge to others. Because communication is conceived on the basis of a common understanding, crass forms of dogmatizing are ruled out. Communications specifies the transcendental precept "be attentive." It provides the data of theology to those willing to hear the "Good News." This book explores some breakthroughs made by those engaged in various disciplines and in religious bodies so as to highlight GEM-FS' relevance in medical studies and policy-making. Lonergan is very clear about GEM-FS's two phases! One may ask to what extent does this involve a reduplicative feedback operative in these two phases and in Lonergan's overall achievement? At the beginning of *MiT*, Lonergan speaks of a "pecking order" among human disciplines which relegates theology to a no-man's land. Medicine doesn't have to be concerned about this since it is a universally recognized, indispensable discipline. This book explores how, in each of the eight functional specialties, scientists, medical doctors, and scholars might collaborate in a twofold GEM-FS feedback process that seeks, in our case, to integrate medicine within psychic and evolutionary processes—taking into account, as noted, what Lonergan named "emergent probability."

---

12. Lonergan, *MiT*, 132, 357.

III

The First Mediating-Creative Phase in Lonergan's *Method in Theology*

The Roles of the First Four FS in a GEM-FS Approach to Medicine

New kinds of systems and their systematic relations have emerged over time as part of an evolving world order that is both materially and formally dynamic. For instance, living things differ from non-living things not only in the complexity of their material organization, but also formally in being self-organizing so long as they are alive. Higher level schemes and things are not systematically related to lower level schemes and things. In Daly's words, "higher level schemes and things depend non-systematically (probabilistically) on lower level schemes and things for their emergence and survival. The spatial image of levels is meant to convey the dependency relationship of higher on lower levels; however, the levels differ from one another not in terms of spatial relations or extension, but in kind."[1]

---

1. Daly, "GEM Model," 433.

FIRST FUNCTIONAL SPECIALTY: RESEARCH AND GATHERING RELEVANT DATA IN MEDICINE WITH A VIEW TO INTEGRATE MEDICINE WITHIN PSYCHIC AND EVOLUTIONARY PROCESSES

In some of his early writings, Lonergan had focused on reconciling the facts of world order with human freedom. In *Insight*, he took great care to study how insights arise from analyzing scientific data and the relation between the two. As to this relation, Daly notes that

> The relation is not systematic. There is no algorithm for getting the right answer in particular situations, although finding and asking the right question(s) can be approached methodically, both in scientific and in practical terms. Galileo, Newton, and others introduced a new way of understanding science that was remarkably open to development in virtue of generating an ongoing cycle of new data and new questions. They searched for and discovered generalizable and invariant correlations—between distances and durations, between force and mass and distance—that order the universe. But these systematic (or classical) generalizations only determine the possible ordering of events. They do not determine their probable ordering, which statistical investigation seeks to understand—when, where, how often, and under what circumstances they do occur. Nor do these classical and statistical correlations necessarily determine the actual ordering of events.[2]

Still, intelligent researchers can help alert people to the possible ordering of events. For example, in FS 1 on research, one might ask whether efforts to integrate medicine within psychic and evolutionary processes would have helped humans prevent the emergence of the corona pandemic. The world community had been warned to such a possibility by the young virologist Nathan Wolfe who in 2006 began research on how viruses transfer from wild animals to humans. Speculating on recurrent patterns in the emergence of viruses, he began forming a network of research outposts around the globe where potentially devastating viruses were poised to make the jump, such as had happened in the Democratic Republic of Congo with the Ebola virus. His biggest fear was that a pandemic that would encircle the globe. Needless to say, that is what happened with COVID-19. Wolfe had examined the relevant data and began a process of interpretation that should have been followed by others. But this gets us beyond a

---

2. Daly, "GEM Model," 424.

mere one-phase GEM model. It would involve understanding some of the relevant processes of nature, how humans have understood and applied them so as to heal body and spirit with a view to create a better future. This is an illustration of how FS 1 can and should function within a GEM-FS diphase, self-correcting approach to our knowing-doing operations. It is a first step that is implicit in Daly's one-phase approach to GEM and could have been more aptly developed within the eight-step GEM-FS framework. As did Nathan Wolfe, one must gather and correctly interpret the data at hand. Overall, as we shall see, FS 5–8 call for a necessary healing process of conversion if we are to do full justice to Lonergan's diphase method.

Daly's View on Clinical Interaction as Linking Heath Science and the Healing Arts

Daly writes that

> Clinical interaction is the hub linking theory and practice, health science and the healing arts. It functions as a special case of the "self-correcting cycle of learning," an intellectual scheme of recurrence where experience of illness → clinical questions → clinical insights → clinical actions → renewed experience of health. The cycle of clinical interaction, like the self-correcting cycle of learning, functions dynamically and leads to cumulative results.[3]

Daly adds that in order to answer questions arising from the data and experience of illness, clinicians must learn how to apply theoretical knowledge based on health science to the benefit of patients. Relying on Lonergan, Daly points out that over and above knowledge of theory and of concrete circumstances, what is needed are insights linking the two, insights into what laws to select, how to combine them, and what to measure to confirm their applicability. These insights, which Lonergan calls "concrete inferences,"[4] can arise circumstantially or they can be anticipated by creative and constructive insights into ideal or typical processes.

Daly suggests that a theory of clinical interaction based on understanding and developing this type of insight into data might well stimulate a robust clinical pedagogy, emphasizing both interpersonal skill development as well as models of clinical reasoning that foster creativity over and above technical manipulation of disease concepts. Clinical health professionals are involved inter-subjectively as embodied subjects

---

3. Daly, "GEM Model," 148.
4. Lonergan, *Insight*, 70.

with patients at each and every step in the clinical cycle, as distinct from ancillary health professionals who engage the cycle only partially or at a distance. Noting that "Nursing assistants also participate in the full clinical cycle, and although their contribution to clinical insight is limited by virtue of education, their contribution to healing is immense and insufficiently valued by present-day society,"[5] Daly adds that for Lonergan, one's interests and concerns pattern images and data arising at the level of experience:

> I direct my attention differently when I am at home or at work, when I study or cross a busy street. The biologic pattern of experience "converges on" sustenance and reproduction and is in large part nonconscious. The dramatic pattern of experience is the primary pattern of everyday living, dominated by practical concerns. It entails the interface of intersubjective communication as well as the interface of conscious with pre-conscious operations within the subject, which Lonergan calls "neural demand functions.[6]

For Daly, social and religious health involves intellectual patterns of experience, including "symbolic, common sense and theoretical knowing."[7] The point that he wants to make is that "Clinical health professionals work to restore healthy schemes of recurrence within a patient's dramatic pattern of experience, while social workers and chaplains work to restore healthy functioning within consciously-mediated social and religious patterns of experience."[8] Daly concludes that "the healing arts are skilled practices, based on common sense and drawing on the theory of health science, intended to improve the health of a particular patient or group of patients. The success of modern science has tended to devalue common sense knowing as "subjective," or as limited to "ordinary attentive sensing. . . . In this view, in order to know something truly we have to put on the scientist's glasses and see its inner constituents."[9] For Lonergan, this indicates an oversight of insight. For example, "when learning to read, the immediate sensible awareness of letters is one thing; the meaning of the letters, invisible but known by the successful reader, is something else. "That something else is the operation of intelligence leading to insights into data."[10] Daly continues:

5. Daly, "GEM Model," 148.
6. See Lonergan, *Insight*, 205–12.
7. Daly, "GEM Model," 149.
8. Daly, "GEM Model," 150.
9. Daly, "Theory of Health Science," 153, referring to Flanagan, *Quest for Self-Knowledge*.
10. Daly, "Theory of Health," 153.

> Knowing the real is knowing the concrete, not only as sensible and particular, but also comprehensively in all its aspects. This requires integrating common sense with theoretical knowing, which is at the heart of the cycle of clinical interaction. Starting with description of the patient's illness in terms of signs and symptoms, the clinician moves to explain the illness in terms of a diagnosis based on medical theory, then to determine and carry out a course of therapy based on this theory. The movement is from concrete to general and back again to concrete. It is unified by insights into intelligible relations between data, theory and action. Such insights add to common sense descriptions and images, so that the common sense of healthcare in 1950 is not the common sense of healthcare in 2008.[11]

Daly's summary provides a good transition point for interpreting various medical views.

2. SECOND FUNCTIONAL SPECIALTY: BEYOND DALY'S VIEWS ON MEDICAL NOTIONS OF INTERPRETATION

Referring to articles by Edmund Pellegrino, David Thomasma, and Daniel Sulmasy, Daly argues that

> The problems facing medicine, practical and theoretical, cut across some of the most pressing and intractable problems facing human society in our time. The authors that I mention stand out in daring to think that these questions can be addressed in a comprehensive way and in laying groundwork for such a comprehensive approach. I contend that Bernard Lonergan's 'critical realism' can buttress these philosophical foundations in a way that is objectively normative and historically dynamic.

The authors here cited by Daly are well beyond the limitations inherent in Hood-Flores's views of interpretation and proactive P4 medicine (quantifying wellness and demystifying disease) that, as we saw, Daly rightly criticizes. Still, one may ask why Daly, who relies on Lonergan's model, has not more fully revised and extended Hood-Flores's notion of interpretation along the lines suggested by Lonergan in *MiT*'s second FS, interpretation.

---

11. Daly, "Theory of Health," 153.

Broadening the Base for Interpreting Medicine and Healthcare

To broaden the perspectives of medical doctors' interpretations of their calling still further, it will be helpful to examine how in the nineteenth century, commentators on evolution revised Darwin's theory by appealing to the study of genetics initiated by Gregor Mendel. Mendel's meticulous experimentation cross-breeding pea plants resulted in evidence for a previously unknown mechanism for heredity. Darwin had struggled with the problem of how organisms pass on traits to their offspring. Why did some traits seem to be passed on and others not? How did the traits of the parents work together in the offspring—did they compete, or combine? Mendel's work helped answer these questions. Unfortunately, Darwin was unaware of Mendel's work during his lifetime. To decode the human genome, scientists today use high-tech methods to view the microscopic chromosomes and even pluck individual genes out of a cell. But in Darwin's time, it was impossible to see any of that. No one was sure how animals or plants passed on their traits. Darwin knew that the lack of an explanation for heredity left a big gap in his theory of natural selection. (See FS 3 below).

Darwin, like many of his contemporaries, speculated that characteristics of the parents were blended—like mixing paint—as they passed to the offspring. But if that were true, some of Darwin's critics pointed out, then how could a single fortunate mutation be spread through a species? It would be blended out, just as a single drop of white paint would be in a gallon of black. Darwin's theory of evolution, which included the familiar principles of mutation, variation, and natural selection, was not readily accepted in his day. Darwin first conceived of his theory when traveling as a naturalist on board the HMS Beagle (1831–36). His contemporary Alfred Russel Wallace had reached a conclusion similar to his. Darwin's theory specified that plants and animals produce more individuals than nature can sustain in each generation. The individuals better suited to their environment are more likely to survive and give their features to future generations. In his *The Origins of Species by Means of Natural Selection* (1859), Darwin wrote that "The laws governing inheritance are for the most part unknown. No one can say why the same peculiarity in different individuals of the same species, or in different species, is sometimes inherited and sometimes not so."[12] Such uncertainty led to, among other interpretations, the now discredited theory of Social Darwinism that individuals, groups, and peoples are subject to the same laws of natural selection as plants and animals. Social Darwinism was used in the late nineteenth

---

12. Darwin, *Origin of Species*, 13.

and twentieth centuries to justify imperialism and racism and to discourage reform.

One may ask why Daly, who relies on Lonergan's model, does not adapt Hood's rather naive notion of interpretation along the lines suggested by Lonergan in *MiT*'s second FS, "Interpretation." Of course, Lonergan's FS2 is concerned about interpreting texts—not medical symptoms. My concern here is to link interpretation with such historical givens as the study of genetics, and to draw the applicable lessons from such a linkage. To do so, let me refer to the example of the origin of the coronavirus and the way it is transmitted—which is still unclear at time of this writing. One hint comes from Theodosius Dobzhansky who distinguished between microevolution and macroevolution in the 1930s. In 1973, he wrote that "Nothing in biology makes sense except in the light of evolution."[13] In 2003, biology professor Michael Dini argued: "The central, unifying principle of biology is the theory of evolution. How can someone who does not accept the most important theory in biology expect to properly practice in the medical field that is so heavily based on biology?"[14]

Recent Analyses of RNA and Links with SARVS-CoV-2

On March 17, 2020, *Nature Medicine* published an analysis of RNA proteins in a variety of coronaviruses, where it was concluded that "our analyses clearly show that SARS-CoV-2 is not a laboratory construct or a purposefully manipulated virus."[15] In his comments, Jonathan Wells stresses that

> first, viruses are not living organisms: They are just pieces of DNA or RNA enclosed in a protein coat. They do not carry out metabolism (the chemical processes that are essential for life), and they do not reproduce themselves (only living cells—or skilled genetic engineers—can make copies of them). Second, even if viruses were considered living things, the evolution of SARS-CoV-2 from another coronavirus would be akin to microevolution—minor changes within existing biological species. ("Species" are not even defined the same way in viruses as they are in living organisms.)[16]

---

13. Dobzhanski, *American Biology Teacher*, 126.
14. Wells, "Coronavirus," para. 11.
15. Wells, "Coronavirus," para. 5.
16. Wells, "Coronavirus," para. 8.

Posing to himself the question of whether SARS-CoV-2 could have evolved from another coronavirus by mutation and natural selection, Wells replies, "I don't see why not, though there is only indirect evidence (from RNA sequences) to support the idea."[17] He added that even if it had happened it would not provide support for Darwinian evolution.

For his part, Jonathan Bartlett, who has studied the logic of design inferences in depth, notes that the authors of the article in *Nature Medicine* discuss the "part of the coronavirus that attaches with very high affinity (very easily) to human ACE2 receptors, . . . [but] that the current software that we use for predicting protein affinity would not have predicted this result."[18] Bartlett does criticize the logic of the study's design inferences—arguing that the scientists had ruled out only one design hypothesis. Therefore, design was still theoretically possible. But Bartlett does not maintain that SARS-CoV-2 is a product of human design.[19]

Yet, the measures being taken against the SARS-CoV-2 pandemic owe nothing to evolutionary theory. In fact, the use of quarantine to block the spread of disease had begun in the fourteenth century. In the 1790s, Edward Jenner began vaccinating people to protect them from smallpox. In 1847, Hungarian obstetrician Ignác Semmelweis demonstrated that proper handwashing lowers mortality from infectious diseases. With such examples of correct interpretation, a pertinent question to ask is how can one's "data of consciousness" be made available to the public sphere—even though they originated in a person in a "private" manner within a person's field of experience? To transpose private acts into a public domain, Lonergan invites each one to empirically examine his/her conscious operations and the mind's process of knowing. His GEM-FS cognitional theory identifies, distinguishes, and relates the sets of acts each person performs to include both data of sense and of consciousness. Let us consider, for example, how this may apply to the history of Mendelian and post-Mendelian genetics from a FS 3 standpoint.

3. THIRD FUNCTIONAL SPECIALTY: A BRIEF HISTORY OF MENDELIAN AND POST-MENDELIAN GENETICS

In the third FS, I consider some of the history that has led to the generally accepted view that takes for granted a sharp divide between facts and values. Darwin's theory of evolution fell out of favor due to the fact that scientists in

---

17. Wells, "Coronavirus," para. 7.
18. Bartlett, "Was the COVID-19 Virus Designed?," para. 2.
19. Wells, "Coronavirus," paras. 8–9.

the late nineteenth century could not reconcile his theory with their understanding of heredity. Paradoxically, Darwin's theory, often a symbol of clash between religion and science, was revived in an alternate form through the work of Gregor Mendel, a devout Roman Catholic friar who took over the monastery's research garden from his mentor, Friar Klacel, in 1846. Klacel had been studying heredity and variation in peas. Mendel would focus on peas as well. This choice was very important to his eventual success. Pea plants have easily identifiable features, can self-fertilize, and are easily prevented from cross-fertilizing. While the choice of pea plant made success more likely, he and his team still had to overcome many hurdles. Mendelian biological inheritance follows the principles originally proposed by Mendel. Michael F. Murray has noted that thanks to Mendel's work, we can now interview a patient in our adult genetics clinic and

> generate a pedigree, track a disease through multiple generations in a family, interpret the pedigree as autosomal dominant..., and then—if we are correct in our interpretation—we can be confident that a single mutated gene is at work in the patient's family. We do not need to know the name of the gene, and in fact often we do not know the name of the gene.[20]

In 1865, after twelve years of systematic investigations on peas, Mendel presented his results in his famous "Versuche über Pflanzenhybriden" which made clear that he had discovered the fundamental laws of inheritance. He concluded that "genes come in pairs and are inherited as distinct units, one from each parent. Mendel tracked the segregation of parent genes and their appearance in the offspring as dominant or recessive traits."[21] Finally, he was able to explain the mathematical patterns of inheritance that occur from one generation to the next. His laws of heredity are usually stated as:

- The Law of Segregation: each inherited trait is defined by a gene pair. Parental genes are randomly separated to the sex cells so that sex cells contain only one gene of the pair. Offspring therefore inherit one genetic allele from each parent when sex cells unite in fertilization.
- The Law of Independent Assortment: genes for different traits are sorted separately from one another so that the inheritance of one trait is not dependent on the inheritance of another.

---

20. Murray, "Mendel," 2.
21. "Johann Gregor Mendel," para. 1.

- The Law of Dominance: an organism with alternate forms of a gene will express the form that is dominant.[22]

Mendel's theory of biological inheritance was at first overlooked but rediscovered and popularized by William Bateson in 1900. It was Bateson who first used the term "genetics" to describe the study of heredity. As noted, Daly commendably rejects approaches to medicine that exclude value from playing any "scientific" role in the study of medicine. With Daly, I seek in Lonergan's work a valid basis for linking values to the science of healing. But I also invoke Lonergan's broad view of "Healing and Creating in History" that insists on the necessity of planetary healing in an age of transformation. Lonergan's notion of global healing necessarily relies on his diphase GEM-FS legacy that takes us beyond a mere "GEM model." By subsuming Daly's notion of a GEM model to the more inclusive notion of GEM-FS process, I seek to show the larger implications and possible applications of Lonergan's broad vision. In effect, the notion of process underlies each of the eight FS—unites them within dynamic self-corrective processes.

The Relation between Monogenetic and Multigenetic Diseases

More than five thousand distinct, monogenic diseases have been clinically described. Researchers and doctors do not always know what gene has caused a particular disease. However in 2009, the value of a new tool for linking Mendelian diseases to their genes was demonstrated. This tool, called "whole exome sequencing" (WES), is widely used in our "genomic era."[23] While WGS (whole genome sequencing) gives information on three billion letters of DNA sequence and is cost-prohibitive and slow, WES gives information on a manageable thirty million letters (1 percent) of DNA sequences. It is cheaper and faster than WGS. At present, WES is just as likely to yield needed answers to the problem of linking genes and diseases.

---

22. "Johann Gregor Mendel," paras. 2–4.
23. Tetreault et al., "Whole-exome Sequencing," 1–12. According to Wikipedia's description, "The exome is composed of all the exons within the genomes, the sequences which, when transcribed, remain within the mature RNA after introns are removed by RNA splicing. This includes untranslated regions of mRNA and coding sequence" ("Exome," para. 1). "Introns are non-coding regions of an RNA's transcript or the DNA encoding it, that are eliminated by splicing before translation" ("Intron," para. 1). Exons go on to be covalently bonded to one another in order to create mature mRNA. In my mRNA-conversion analogue, exons have roles analogous to that of the conversions in the second phase of Lonergan's GEM-FS process method.

Darwin, Teilhard de Chardin, Monod, and Evolution

Intelligent design was not the most serious challenge to Darwin's theory of evolution in its long history. As I previously noted, scientists in the late nineteenth century could not reconcile Darwin's theory with their current understanding of heredity. This flaw was serious enough to cause it to fall out of favor for decades. Paradoxically, Darwin's theory of evolution, often a symbol of the clash of religion and science, was revived and given new impetus through the work of Mendel—a very religious person. Darwin had proposed that, with the natural variations that occur in populations, any trait that is beneficial would make that individual more likely to survive and pass on the trait to the next generation. Natural selection could result in completely new species. Darwin did not have an explanation for how the traits could be preserved over the succeeding generations. At the time, the prevailing theory of inheritance was that the traits of the parents were blended in the offspring. But this would mean that any beneficial trait would be diluted out of the population within a few generations. This is because most of the blending over the next generations would be with individuals that did not have the trait. It was Mendel who came up with an answer to Darwin's problem: traits are not blended, but inherited whole.

The development of neo-Darwinism in the first third of the twentieth century incorporated natural selection with Mendelian genetics. Just as neo-Darwinism seeks to integrate Darwin's theory of evolution by natural selection with Mendel's theory of genetics, so I appeal to Lonergan's diphase method developed in *MiT* to interconnect various problematics facing humanity by adverting to the needed transition points involved in human cognitive-doing aspects of life. An example of this may also be found in Teilhard de Chardin's views on evolution interpreted by some as a process theology or as a theistic framework compatible with GEM-FS.

Hunter Dukes has contrasted the spiritualism implicit in Teilhard de Chardin's noosphere with Jacques Monod's appropriation of the term. Monod was an atheist. He won the Nobel Prize for Physics in 1965 for having helped discover how cells adapt to changes in levels of oxygen and how this can increase our ability to fight global poverty. In his *Chance and Necessity* (1970), Monod argued that the "ultimate aim of science is to clarify man's relationship to the universe."[24] He stressed the importance of the molecular theory of the genetic code—a physical theory of heredity. For him, this "was the second secret of life."[25] As he saw it, molecular biology and

---

24. Monod, *Chance and Necessity*, xi.
25. Fenton, "Allostery," 421.

neurochemistry have both developed Darwinism and modified classical assumptions. It is as if current biology had figured out the very nature of man. One may summarize such diverse developments in biology, chemistry, and genetics by quoting Lonergan's "Healing and Creating in History" which stresses his diphase GEM-FS approach to science and history:

> While it can take a series of disasters to convince people of the need for creating, still the long, hard, uphill climb is the creative process itself. In retrospect, this process may appear as a grand strategy that unfolds in an orderly manner and cumulative series of steps. But any retrospect has the advantage of knowing the answers. The creative task is to find the answers. It is a matter of insight, not of one insight but of many, not of isolated insights but of insights that coalesce, . . . that reveal their shortcomings in their concrete results.[26]

Lonergan goes on say that this calls for psychic and societal healing so as to refashion societal structures. Psychotherapists and psychiatrists can play a role in this to the extent they can help humans live better lives, personally and collectively. Teilhard de Chardin, like Lonergan and Pope Francis, was a Christian visionary. Pope Francis in his *Laudato Si*, draws upon Teilhard's insights. For these three Jesuits, religion and science complement one another. Humanity must take measures to ensure a sustainable future for the planet and its inhabitants. Lonergan's notion of psychic and societal process, as I argue below, can help us integrate the various facets of life in ways scientists and other thinkers have tentatively striven to do in their various ways. The fourth FS tackles such issues in dialectical fashion.

FOURTH FUNCTIONAL SPECIALTY: DIALECTIC AND CARING FOR THE SICK

GEM-FS is a diphase feedback process in which experience, understanding, judgment and dialectic are interrelated, not as in common sense fashion, but in such a way that the ends proper to particular levels "become the objective sought by operations on all four levels." On this topic, Daly poses and answers a question:

> But what are we to make of Lonergan's very words, "experiencing one's experiencing," repeated several times with minor variation in the summary statement of transcendental method? Did he misspeak or was he tacitly engaged in virtue of the tension of

26. Lonergan, "Healing and Creating," 103.

human consciousness with a unity at once precarious and alive? I am pursuing the latter possibility. One important point to keep in mind is that the field of experience—encompassing interior and exterior experience—is unified performatively. A second point is that embodied subjects' wakefulness and attentiveness vary; consciousness is a matter of degree.[27]

Here, Daly's medical viewpoint seems to prevail at the expense of philosophy. He does quote Lonergan's statement in "Understanding and Being:"

> I think there is something very true in the Hegelian connection between the subjective spirit and its manifestation in objective spirit . . . Self-appropriation is conditioned not merely by the fact that one is empirically, intelligently, and rationally conscious; it is conditioned also by that fact as manifested.[28]

Daly's exploration of "the significance of being oneself as a mode of consciousness that is heightened by transcendental method; of feelings as data that are given in this mode of consciousness," etc., does bring him closer to a GEM-FS approach. But what Daly fails to do is to adequately explore Lonergan's notion of horizon and the differences in horizon that Lonergan notes may be complementary, genetic, or dialectical. Daly touches on this latter point, but does not sufficiently explore Lonergan's treatment of "Conversions and Breakdowns."[29] This may explain the point that Daly seems to have missed, namely, that it is possible that acquiring a new horizon "involves an about-face."[30] Michael McCarthy, as we shall see, does not miss that critical point. Only when we get into the second phase of the FS can one speak authentically from one's converted standpoint that transposes the general and special categories and one's horizon. As with our four basic operations, which they reduplicatively implement (see Fig. 1), each of the FS has its own mode of operating and can be treated separately and/or cumulatively. There is, however, a paradox in moving from dialectic to foundations, from *MiT*'s first phase to its second phase, inasmuch as in FS 5 one may have to encounter mysticism, the apophatic, the world of interiority—what is beyond words even when dealing with people's psychological dispositions and with pastoral problems. In *MiT*'s chapter 4 on "Religion," Lonergan speaks of self-transcendence as one of the problems Kierkegaard struggled with and about which he wrote much. One might say that Kierkegaard was not so

---

27. Daly, "Transcendental Method in Action," 3.
28. Lonergan, "Understanding and Being," *CWL* 5, 219.
29. Lonergan, *MiT*, 243.
30. Lonergan, *MiT*, 236.

much interested in our lives' "knowing part" as he was with the paradoxes sensitive people cannot but feel in the face of life's many contradictions and injustices. How bridge such "gaps?"

In FS 4, dialectic, Lonergan goes into our mental acts and the realms of meaning, concluding: the conditions "for using mental acts as a logical first are numerous. If one insists on remaining in the world of common sense and ordinary language . . . , one's decisions preclude the possibility of entering into the world of interiority."[31] But when the three realms of common sense, theory, and interiority are differentiated, the self-appropriation of the subject leads to objectifying "the four basic acts of religious experience."[32] Lonergan's view on mental acts and on the secondary qualities' validity are a key to understanding how he helps us reconcile and integrate the interior facets of our lives so that we may live in authentic ways for the good of all. Through such authentic living, the legitimate relations between science and ethics can be addressed transculturally. GEM-FS depends not on swashbuckling heroes who would right human wrongs; rather, it seeks to unite thinking people and help link, even organize them to the extent possible in functionally specialized ways based on the effective implementation of the conversions. It is in such ways that GEM-FS can help foster transcultural-interfaith dialogues by countering propaganda and oppression.

GEM-FS's dialectical structure (based on the pattern of our related and recurrent operations) develops differently in converted investigators able to distinguish counter-positions from positions.[33] Those who have not experienced conversion will have only a notional apprehension of such a process. One must first understand the operational range and assumptions of dialogue partners. One must give the benefit of the doubt while remaining within a critical, charitable mode. While GEM-FS seeks the best ways to communicate, one must realize that no person, no approach is perfect. Persons are subject to an ongoing process of further conversions—of better appropriating one's four basic operations. The structure of dialectic occurs on an upper level and a lower one. On the upper level, there are the two operators or precepts whereby one develops positions and reverses counter-positions. "Positions are statements compatible with intellectual, moral and religious conversion."[34] Counter-positions are not compatible with such conversions. One must develop positions and reverse what is incompatible with conversion. Before operating on the statements in the lower level of

31. Lonergan, *MiT*, 262.
32. Lonergan, *MiT*, 266.
33. Lonergan, *MiT*, 251.
34. Lonergan, *MiT*, 249.

dialectic, one must assemble, complete, compare, reduce, classify and select the relevant material. This entails the different horizons within which investigators operate. If investigators' horizons differ, further objectifications of horizons are in order. Let us consider, for example, how the Enlightenment's stress on secular values upset the traditional applecart but promoted science.

How the European Enlightenment Revised Views on the Nature of Science

In his "New Critical Center," Michael McCarthy reflects on Pascal's aphorism that "Unity without multiplicity is tyranny, multiplicity without unity is confusion."[35] He notes that Lonergan consistently appealed "for a critical cultural center that avoids both the classicist's predilection for a restrictive unity and the relativist's surrender to pluralistic confusion."[36] McCarthy then reminds us that the European Enlightenment, besides creating new scientific theories and disciplines, fundamentally revised our understanding of the nature of science. The classicist conception of science elaborated in Aristotle's *Posterior Analytics* envisaged science as a permanent propositional achievement, expressing true, certain knowledge of causal necessity. For Aristotelians, once the basic principles of knowledge were discovered, they could serve as the axiomatic base for an ordered series of rigorous inferences. However, McCarthy notes that for Lonergan,

> The modern, empirical notion of science significantly modifies each of the defining features of classical episteme. Scientific inquiry is now understood as a collective and historical process whose unifying center is not a permanent set of un-revisable propositions but a common reliance on empirical method. And these propositions are no longer seen as immutable truths, but as the articulate expression of the existing state of scientific understanding. The central point is not simply that we know more about nature than our classical predecessors did, but that we understand the disciplined practice of investigating nature in a fundamentally different way.[37]

McCarthy is here referring to an article Lonergan had written several years after *Insight* as he was then busy writing *MiT*. McCarthy observes that,

---

35. McCarthy, "Critical Center," 113.
36. McCarthy, "Critical Center," 115.
37. McCarthy, "Critical Center," 117.

in this time period, Lonergan began to insist that while complementary and genetic differences can be effectively integrated, the numerous instances of dialectical pluralism cannot. "They represent mutually inconsistent basic and irreducible intentional oppositions. These oppositional conflicts are the appropriate concern of Lonergan's dialectical method whose goal is to bring fundamental disagreements to light to exhibit their originating grounds in intentional consciousness, and to resolve their rivalry through critical judgments and authentic decisions."[38] An analogical process occurred, as we saw in the transition from Mendel to post-Mendelian concepts of heredity. Dialectic helps resolve rival claims through critical judgments and authentic decisions. The positions and counter positions of cognitional theory, epistemology, and metaphysics exhibit a crucial dialectical polarity:

> In the field of ethics, the contrasting notions of the good, before and after moral conversion, are also dialectically opposed. In the domain of cultural conflict, dialectical method is needed to distinguish the inauthentic meanings and values rooted in the several forms of human biases from their authentic counterparts rooted in the normative eros and exigency of intentional cooperation.[39]

McCarthy concludes his remarks on Dialectic, by noting that for Aristotle, nature and art are distinct but complementary principles of change. Lonergan, on the other hand, appeals to the human spirit to distinguish between nature and art. This leads to a different emphasis:

> As art imitates and completes the operations of nature, so violence distorts and destroys them. In Aquinas' systematic theology, nature and grace are complementary sources of the human good, while sin in its various modes is a principle of violence, weakening our natural created tendencies and requiring the healing action of redemptive grace. Within Lonergan's third stage intentional analysis, Aristotle's metaphysical principle of natural form is transposed into the eros and exigency of the human spirit, while the categories of violence and sin become different sources of polarizing bias and intentional impotence.[40]

For McCarthy, the reason for a detailed historical retrieval is to deepen our understanding of the contemporary cultural situation and to promote a critical engagement with it. In our age of a global culture permeated by

---

38. McCarthy, "Critical Center," 125, referring to *MiT*, 249–53.
39. McCarthy, "Critical Center," 111.
40. McCarthy, "Critical Center," 125, referring to Aristotle's *Physics*.

change and diversity, the natural and human sciences continue their dynamic growth, but

> Our political and social institutions are struggling to adapt. We have lost a common moral ontology, a unifying anthropological and religious framework within which to make sense of our lives; and our cultural innocence has been shattered by an unprecedented theoretical and scholarly effort to understand ways of life that are historically remote and spatially distant. We have come gradually, and often haltingly, to a new awareness and acceptance of pluralism. But where do these momentous changes leave the individual person, the emerging existential subject? It is irresponsible to judge prior to understanding, but there is far too much for any single person to understand; and pressing judgments and decisions will not wait upon a life of disinterested inquiry.[41] This has led young people to grope towards maturity but "the alternating shrillness and inarticulacy of their elders have made them skeptical of objectivity and suspicious of nearly all moral claims and aspirations."[42]

Locating the Invariant Critical Norms with the Help of Cardinal Newman and of Engineers

A crucial philosophical point concerns the location of the invariant critical norms that affect objectivity. Classicists insist on the need for transcultural principles in the antifoundational climate promoted by historicism. But they fail to grasp the type of foundational principles appropriate to the present. It is for such reasons that Lonergan developed his FS approach in *MiT* to complement and transpose his GEM-standpoint elaborated in *Insight*. Lonergan calls us to follow Cardinal Newman in going beyond "a notional apprehension of conversion" to one based on one's personal, actual experience of intellectual, moral, and religious conversions.[43] Lonergan briefly retraces the history of philosophy that has led to many types of confusion such as that of naïve realists and the naïve idealism that led to Kant, to the absolute idealism of Hegel etc. His basic interest in dialectic is whether a person "has undergone intellectual, moral, and religious conversion."[44] Because they are based on the type of invariant critical norms elaborated

---

41. McCarthy, "Critical Center," 126.
42. McCarthy, "Critical Center," 127.
43. Lonergan, *MiT*, 251.
44. Lonergan, *MiT*, 251.

in Lonergan's spelling out of the virtually unconditioned, the FS enable collaborative efforts to address the present age's tendency to be dominated by skepticism or distrust. These latter are characterized by futile searches for foundations in logic or by mistaken forms of metaphysics. Lonergan, on the other hand, has shown that logic, ethics, and other disciplines require a foundation in human nature which is concrete, dynamic, empirical, and rooted in intentionality. He argued that when the natural and the human sciences are on the move, and when the everyday dimensions of culture are changing, "what is needed is not a dam to block the stream of change, but critical control of the riverbed through which the stream must flow."[45]

Lonergan's shift to empirical method is one that is dynamically methodological. Concepts do not emerge from a closed, totalizing and all-encompassing system. GEM-FS is open to all relevant data; it takes into account existential acts. Unlike a dialectical-necessitarian approach, Lonergan's method demands that new data be gleaned from all sources, be attended to and appropriated in some way. Daly's rather skimpy treatment of the underlying Cartesian-Enlightenment issues emphasized by McCarthy and others such as Charles Taylor needs to be addressed. Daly does decry the modern tendency to divorce values from science, but he does not sufficiently investigate how Lonergan helps us remedy this lack in his treatment of the last four FS. Medically speaking, these consist of foundations (FS 5), the ramifications of nature systems in contemporary thought and practice (FS 6) and in policy-making (FS 7), as well as how best to efficiently communicate the implications of e. g. new medicines and medical treatments.

Here, let us invoke *MiT*'s chapter 5 where Lonergan says in sec. 4 that there is a need for division among the eight FS. Rather than engaging in "long-standing controversial and apologetic types of theology" of former days, his method clearly points to "The Need for Division." What is new in his conception of the branches of theology as FS is that they are "distinct and separate stages in a single process from data to results."[46] Sec. 5 named, "A Dynamic Unity," stresses the dynamic aspects of this unity. Later, he specifies that in the realm of interiority, "Language speaks . . .of the subject and his operations as objects but, nonetheless, rests upon a self-appropriation that has verified in personal experience the operator, the operations, and the processes referred to in the basic terms and relations of the language employed."[47] Let me here appeal to an engineer and to a philosopher who have jointly published an article in which they apply Lonergan's method to

---

45. Lonergan, "Future of Thomism," 47.
46. Lonergan, *MiT*, 136.
47. Lonergan, *MiT*, 257.

engineering. They examine the nature of engineering design as activities of knowing and willing. They argue that Lonergan "offers a knowing-based approach with the flexibility needed for an epistemology of the many-sided activity of engineering."[48] They conclude that, in effect, the activities in which we engage conform to objectified data and can be repeated at will; these activities constitute the knowledge reference inasmuch as any experiment has a concrete referent.

The Role of Operators in GEM-FS Process

Operators are one of the key, integrative notions in the entire "GEM-FS" enterprise, but they are seldom addressed systematically even by Lonergan's students. In Lonergan's opus, the notion of operator first appears in *Insight*, chapter 15 where he notes that the operator, is in the general case, "the upwardly directed dynamism of proportionate being of what he has named 'finality.'"[49] He adds that among other functions, "operators form a flexible series along which the organism advances from the generic functioning of the initial cell to the flexible circle of ranges of schemes of the mature type."[50]

Adequate Transition Points between Lonergan's Mediating-Creating and Mediated-Healing Phases in *MiT*.

On this topic, I wish to make five basic points. The first regards Lonergan's treatment of development and psychic process; the second addresses the realm of interiority; the third concerns Martin Buber's insights into "I-Thou" dialogue; the fourth touches on the German use of praxis in medicine. The fifth compares Lonergan's notion of process with Alfred North Whitehead's notion of process theology.

1. *Human Development and Psychic Process*

Underlying Lonergan's notion of development and psychic process, there is a principle of emergence according to which otherwise coincidental manifolds (random or chance juxtapositions) of lower conjugates acts invite higher integrations by higher conjugate forms. Further, there is also a principle of correspondence which stipulates that different manifolds

48. Frezza and Nordquest, "Engineering Insight," 22.
49. Lonergan, *Insight*, 490.
50. Lonergan, *Insight*, 491.

of underlying events require different higher integrations.[51] Different chemical elements, for example, have different atomic numbers grounded in the differing underlying manifolds while different aggregates of aggregates of chemical processes involve different organisms, etc.

Daly rightly argues that Lonergan provides an account of explanatory genera and species in *Insight*, whereby "chemical elements and compounds are higher integrations of otherwise coincidental manifolds of subatomic events. In turn, organisms are higher integrations of otherwise coincidental manifolds of chemical processes; sensitive consciousness is a higher integration of otherwise coincidental manifolds of changes in neural tissues; and accumulating insights are higher integrations of otherwise coincidental manifolds of images or of data."[52]

Daly writes that Lonergan distinguishes systematic and non-systematic processes in his account of world order, which he calls emergent probability. Their combined unfolding allows for the emergence of generically distinct levels of schemes and things in *world process*, "characterized by distinct systematic relations at each level, the statistical dependence of higher level schemes and things on lower-level schemes and things, and the setting of internal boundaries."[53] One may ask why Daly has not picked up on the fact that, as suggested by this passage, for Lonergan, world process underlies and is primary to a "GEM model"?

As to Lonergan's treatment of human development as a psychic process, it is illustrated in the section of *Insight* on "Human Development."[54] There, he stresses that in humans, "organic, psychic, and intellectual development are not three independent processes. They are interlocked, with the intellectual providing a higher integration of the psychic and the psychic providing a higher integration of the organic. Each level involves its own laws."[55]

It is important to note that Daly's relying on "interlocking sets of terms and relations" to support his "GEM model" should be considered as part of the higher integration of psychic process—which, in fact, underlies Daly's GEM model. In reality, his model is that of world and psychic processes which Lonergan expounded throughout his career and developed at length in the functional specialization process of *MiT*.

---

51. Lonergan, *Insight*, 555.
52. Morelli and Morelli, *Lonergan Reader*, 249.
53. Daly, "GEM Model," 421.
54. Lonergan, *Insight*, 494–504.
55. Lonergan, *Insight*, 494.

Yet, Daly confuses or does not advert to the difference between two sets of interlocking sets of terms and relations used by Lonergan. The "interlocking set of terms and relations" which informs Daly's model presupposes the set of the GEM-FS process operations which I have been stressing. Daly's GEM model would be more effective when taken as a GEM-FS process model to avoid any static residues. In *MiT*, Lonergan develops the eight FS on the model of a feedback set of interlocking terms and relations. It enables a GEM-FS process of transformative operations that people and even profound thinkers tend to take for granted. Lonergan took pains to show why we should be attentive, intelligent, rational and responsible. Needless to say, my efforts to integrate our human psychic-intellectual processes within evolutionary realities parallel Daly's efforts. But I stress the need to identify the precise transition points that enable Lonergan scholars to move from the mediating-creating phase to the foundations of GEM-FS's mediated-healing phase. Being precise about these transition points is important, for example, when considering medicine as adapting to new medical quandaries-breakthroughs. Here, pertinent examples can be invoked. A straightforward but tragic example is that of the young Chinese doctor who designed two baby girls by editing their DNA.[56] Another example regards the ethical implications of assisted suicides. In both cases, not all that is feasible in medicine is moral or ethical.[57]

2. *The Realm of Interiority*

A second transition point touches on the realm of interiority which Lonergan addresses in *MiT*. In this realm, language speaks of the subject and his/her operations as objects. But this rests "upon a self-appropriation that has verified in personal experience the operator, the operations, and the processes referred to in the basic terms and relations of the language employed."[58] Here, one must stress the fact that Lonergan writes about these processes at the end of his treatment of FS4, dialectic, in which he emphasizes, for example, that just as "there are two meanings of the word, object, so too there are two meanings of the word, objectivity:

---

56. He Jiankui announced in November 2018 that he had used a powerful technique (CRISPR) on a human embryo to edit the genes of twin girls. He said he modified a gene intending to protect the girls against HIV, the virus that causes AIDS. He was sentenced to three years in jail for illegal practice.

57. More theoretical, scholarly examples are those illustrated in Michel Foucault's *Order of Things*.

58. Lonergan, *MiT*, 257.

In the world of immediacy the necessary and sufficient condition of objectivity is to be a successfully functioning animal. But in the world mediated by meaning objectivity has three components. There is the experiential objectivity constituted by the givenness of the data of sense and the data of consciousness. There is the normative objectivity constituted by the exigencies of intelligence and reasonableness. There is the absolute objectivity that results from combining the results of experiential and normative objectivity so that through experiential objectivity conditions are fulfilled while through normative objectivity conditions are linked to what they condition.[59]

3. A Philosophy of Personal Dialogue

A third transition point, closely related to the previous one, is Martin Buber's insights into an I-Thou exchange which present us with a philosophy of personal dialogue. Buber describes how personal dialogue can help us define the nature of reality itself. For him, human existence may be defined by the way in which we engage in dialogue with one another, with the world, and with God. Humans can adopt either of two attitudes toward another person: I-thou or I-it. While an I-thou attitude relates persons to one another as subject-to-subject, an I-it stance reduces him/her to being an object. In the I-thou relationship, human beings are aware of each other as having a unity of being; they do not perceive each other as consisting of specific, isolated qualities, but engage in a dialogue involving each other's "*whole* being."[60] In I-it relationships, on the other hand, human beings perceive one another as consisting of specific, isolated qualities: they reduce one another to being parts of the world of things. "I-thou is a relationship of mutuality and reciprocity, while I-it is a relationship of separateness and detachment."

The Hasidic tradition (of which he had lost sight as a young man) informs Buber's thought. His re-encounter with Hasidism meant for him a re-entry into tradition. Tradition is not just a matter of preserving the past; we must also pass it on. The root idea of Hasidism is that God takes his dwelling-place within humans and within his creation. This idea is not peculiar to Hasidism for it is already contained in a Torah text which reads: "I will put my dwelling place among you, and I will not abhor you. I will walk among you and be your God, and you will be my people" (Lev 26:11–12). For Buber, this came to mean the actual annulment of the difference between

---

59. Lonergan, *MiT*, 263.
60. Buber, *I and Thou*, 67.

religiousness and secularity. This is also an issue, a challenge that should be addressed by Christians, Muslims, and believers in other traditions. To deal with this issue, I take the liberty to rephrase Buber's I-thou relationship into a tripartite "I-thou-Thou," one that includes God's role in our lives so as to underpin "I-thou" relations—as also suggested in *MiT*. This rephrasing is, I think, consistent with Buber's view of dialogue. Buber felt compelled to write, but writing was not the most important part of his life. The most important part of his life was his relationship with others. For him, the analogy of the chrysalis and the butterfly[61] teaches us to meet others and to hold our ground when we meet them. In this passage, he stressed that the most important or essential, is the word "teaches." "It takes a lifetime to learn how to be able to hold your own ground, to go out to the others, to be open to them without losing your ground. And to hold your ground without shutting others out."[62]

Buber spoke of three kinds of dialogue: 1) genuine dialogue, in which each of the participants really has in mind the other or others in their present and particular being; 2) technical dialogue, prompted solely by the need of objective understanding; 3) monologue, disguised as dialogue, in which two or more men, meeting in space, speak each with himself in strangely tortuous and circuitous ways and yet imagine they have escaped the torment of being thrown back on their own resources. Buber did not accept absolute formulas for living. "No preconceived code can see ahead to everything that can happen in a man's life. As we live, we grow and our beliefs change. They must change. So I think we should live with this constant discovery. We should be open to this adventure in heightened awareness of living: we should stake our whole existence on our willingness to explore."[63]

4. The Long History of the Word "Praxis" and its Various Notions

A fourth aspect of adequate transition points between Lonergan's mediating-creating and mediated-healing phases in *MiT* notes the difference in the contemporary use and meaning of the word praxis in the German and English languages. Praxis in the modern German idiom refers primarily to a medical practice or that of a dentist or veterinarian. But in philosophy, "praxis" has a long history going back to Aristotle. The word has been used by Hegel, Marx, and Kierkegaard in what amounts to contradictory ways, confusing it with "action." Richard J. Bernstein has noted that the action

---

61. Buber, *I and Thou*, 69.
62. Martin Buber, quoted in "Dipti Gupta," para. 1.
63. Quoted in Hobes, *Buber*, 56.

"involved in passionately choosing an existential possibility is not measured by any external criteria; it is the decisiveness and action of inwardness. Although Kierkegaard's *Climacus* agreed with the Hegelian and Marxist formula that a man is what he does, *Climacus*'s specification of what this formula means is anti-Hegelian and anti-Marxist. "All the themes that we have been tracing in Kierkegaard's writings culminate in [the] conception of action as inward decision and the demand that each of us must choose what he is to become."[64]

In reality, Bernstein tells us, Kierkegaard "seeks to show us that all choice, decisiveness, and action leads to despair. . . . Kierkegaard's 'existential dialectic' leads in a curious and desperate way to an overwhelming sense of our own impotence,"[65] needing a leap of faith. Be that as it may, Catholic, Christian teaching has inspired many doctors in medicine to live their faith and practice in hope, not despair. Thankfully, there are in the world various Catholic and Christian medical associations which seek to build bridges between physical and spiritual healing. They organize meetings and publish to meet these ends. For his part, Pope Francis has affirmed that Catholic doctors have a mission to show God's compassionate love to those who are suffering and to defend life at all stages.[66]

5. Comparing the Dynamics of Alfred N. Whitehead's Notion of Process Theology with the Insights of Zen Buddhism, Bernard Lonergan, and Thomas Merton

In order to give as wide a context as possible for relating views on healing, I here attempt to situate Lonergan's work within larger contexts that Lonergan himself had to tackle to make GEM-FS relevant to world traditions and to experimental theologies. As noted throughout this text, conversations between theology, medicine, and psychology are often constrained by a series of seemingly intractable difficulties due to various competing assumptions about empirical verification etc. Let me first invoke Thomas E. Hosinski's remarks on process theology:

> Almost all philosophers and theologians who have addressed process theology have understood Lonergan's philosophy of God to be at odds with the interpretation of God presented by Alfred North Whitehead or Charles Hartshorne. It is difficult

---

64. Bernstein, *Praxis*, 116.
65. Bernstein, *Praxis*, 117.
66. See Francis, "Address to the International Federation."

to disagree with this stance—and difficult to envision any other type of discussion—so long as we confine ourselves to Lonergan's conscious intention, his stated philosophy of God in *Insight*, and his own judgment [that] . . . his philosophy of God is at odds with a process understanding of God.[67]

Despite this state of affairs, Hosinski addresses this topic in an original manner. He does not directly compare Lonergan's philosophy of God with Whitehead's nor does he venture into debating their relative merits. Rather, his concern is entirely with the inner dynamics of Lonergan's own thought. He views the implications of the developments in Lonergan's post-*Insight* thought as having influenced his philosophy of God. "Although they have been applied to the context in which the philosophy of God is done, [the implications] have yet to be applied fully to Lonergan's understanding of God that results"[68] from his various inquires. Hosinski proposes "the novel and unexpected thesis that Lonergan's thought can be a resource for a process understanding of God."[69] He adds that Whitehead, in his *Religion in the Making*, speaks of the creative process as "focusing the universe into one unity. It survives because the universe is a process of attaining instances of definite experience out of its own elements."[70]

For her part, Kathleen Fischer cites Lonergan's remark that his philosophy of God expressed in *Insight* was marked by a key incongruity. In his words, this consisted in the fact that "While my cognitional theory was based on a long and methodical appeal to experience, in contrast, my account of God's existence and attributes made no appeal to religious experience."[71] While Lonergan's views on process thought need further clarification, my focus on Lonergan's approaches to cosmological and psychological processes seeks to provide a background—see also Appendix D and some of my previous writings on Buddhism which have sought to find the experiential-foundational bridging aspects of Buddhism, notably those of Zen Buddhism as approached by Thomas Merton. Merton has been held up as a modern mystic, a model of authenticity, who helped bridge some of the chasms secularity has set between the sacred and the secular aspects of our lives. Converted at the age of twenty-two from his relentless pursuit of pleasure, he eventually stressed in his many writings the primacy of

---

67. Hosinski, "Process Understanding of God," para. 1.
68. Hosinski, "Process Understanding of God," para. 2.
69. Hosinski, "Process Understanding of God," para. 2.
70. Whitehead, *Religion in the Making*, 108.
71. Morelli and Morelli, *Lonergan Reader*, 222.

religious experience so as to reconcile the spiritual strivings of Christianity and Zen Buddhism.

What may be of great relevance for solving such modern dilemmas as to the compatibility between the spiritual and material dimensions of our lives and the need to bridge these dimensions is the notion of the void, of nothingness apprehended by Buddhist, Christian, and Sufi mystics and to some extent clarified by Lonergan. Such apprehension of "the void" involves a spiritual process with creating-healing phases which I shall consider in more detail below.

Summarizing Part III's Attempt to Clear the Ground for the Mediated-Healing Phase

In Part III, I have examined how the first four FS are consonant with Daly's project. However, I have insisted that his project, if it is to be effective and meet his hopes for a "GEM model," should also clearly draw the full implications of Lonergan's GEM-FS achievement. Consonant with Matthew Lamb's emphasis on genuine Christian praxis (one which is theoretically informed), I have stressed the importance of carefully balancing one's theorizing with a genuine Christian ethical, spiritual praxis. It is against this background and with this aim in mind that, in Part IV, I specify the indispensable, complementary roles of the last four FS which are needed if one is to build interdisciplinary, ethical bridges that can meet our spiritual and social needs. This is why, for example, FS 6 addresses the issues and policies involved in implementing health care today while FS 7 examines how communities can best deal with systemic shortcomings in healthcare. With this in mind, I turn to examine some of the main roles of the last four FS in Lonergan's GEM-FS process method with the intention of relating these roles to their spiritually-morally healing functions in our lives.

IV

The Second Mediated-Healing Phase in Lonergan's *Method in Theology*[1]

The Indispensable Roles of the Last Four Functional Specialties in MiT

Part IV develops some central arguments to show how Daly's failure to account for the full potential of Lonergan's method can be remedied by addressing some of the further implications of "GEM-FS process" rather than restricting the method to a mere GEM model.

A GEM-FS process method is an appropriate, encompassing way to integrate and expand Daly's model within process categories that include

---

1. Friedrich Nietzsche wrote about the re-evaluation ("trans-valuation") of values. Parts III and IV evaluate and apply Lonergan's helpful hints as to how we can go about re-evaluating such issues.

evolutionary[2] and psychic processes.[3] Daly's single-phase GEM model undercuts GEM's full potential which can only be realized through a diphase GEM-FS-process approach. Such a diphase approach includes Lonergan's original approach to operators. As noted above, the difficulty in studying the operators lies in the complexity of their data. With Phil McShane, I rely on Lonergan's simpler view of operator developed in *MiT*. This simpler view of operator (which I applied in FS 4) is a serious forward-speaking, a direct speaking. We cannot just remain with the givens of our operations; we have to get into the givens of applied operators in various fields and their operational processes both physical and psychic.[4] As we saw, Lonergan stresses that in the realm of interiority, language speaks of the subject and his/her operations as objects. This rests "upon a self-appropriation that has verified in personal experience the operator, the operations, and the processes referred to in the basic terms and relations of the language employed."[5] It is due to such a verification process that one can then move on to genuinely authentic[6] foundations—to the second healing phase of the GEM-FS transformative process method anchored in the various conversions.

---

2. For Lonergan, there are two types of cosmology. The first speaks of universal propositions, self-evident truths; the second appeals to nature not as abstractly conceived but as concretely operating. Lonergan stresses the latter for it helps determine norms within historical contexts. If one asks how does the world operate concretely and what operations and norms ground human progress, one is led to emergent probability which is a "conditioned series of things and schemes" within a series that is realized cumulatively in accord with successive schedules of probabilities" (Lonergan, *Insight*, 290). It is a series which differs from Darwin's account and which also stands in opposition to determinism and indeterminism. It is what allows us to transform the world with the perspective of historical mindedness.

3. Psychic process may involve an intention with a particular place in a series of content-related representations, strivings, decisions, etc. In some cases, two intentions may be at work: a manifest intention which has failed and a latent intention which caused the failure. We must avoid the pretensions of modernity through the differentiation of interiority and a new integration of the spiritual, the intellectual, the moral, and the historical aspects of life.

4. See Dunne, "Bernard Lonergan." Implied here is a profound change of horizon, whereby a spiritual-ethical life becomes normative.

5. Lonergan, *MiT*, 257.

6. Lonergan in *Insight* speaks of genuineness. *MiT* addresses the existential aspects of authenticity.

FIFTH FUNCTIONAL SPECIALTY: REINSTATING THE *AUTHENTIC FOUNDATIONS* MANY OVERLOOK[7] THROUGH A BROADENING OF TRANSFORMATIVE PROCESS HORIZONS

A General Perspective on "Changes of Mind" Involved in Doing Science

Sets of questions are related to each other. Some sets are related to empirical facts in the natural world, including questions related to how humans have tampered with or destroyed nature's own evolutionary structures. Another set is germane to human economic choices and their effects on underlying natural processes. Beyond such sets of questions there are further ones about the very inner "light" enabling one to ask questions in the first place. Here, the ethical question arises as to how we can best address these issues—namely "what ought we be doing?" We are here touching on basic questions for FS 5, foundations. Lonergan asks religious people to think about foundations in the light of faith and scientists to think in the light of the scientific method—which also includes beliefs. Scientists tend to believe other scientists. They believe because they cannot reproduce all experiments conducted by other scientists.[8] Lonergan often emphasized the role that belief plays in daily life but also in scientific practice. The scientific process is not independent of beliefs because scientists must believe the valid results of experiments conducted by others. Beliefs are also involved in reaching any probably warranted assertion which involves a long, tortuous social and communitarian process. Sound policies in medicine and healthcare depend on beliefs but may also result in transforming previously held beliefs. Such transformations occur due to empirical tests and communal assessments.

---

7. Daly, in a private message, indicated to me that he is "intentionally working in the specialty foundations." The heart of his model is based on the intrapersonal levels of subjective and organic functioning based on Lonergan's interpersonal structure of the human good. It is a model of health, not medicine. He began with the idea that health is a subset of the human good. He then expanded his notion to take into account the fact that "nature heals." He argues that "pre-intentional levels of healing emerged long before humans arrived on the scene and these schemes continue to be the foundation of ecological health. Technology is often blind to such foundations." I argue that Daly's view must be complemented with Lonergan's point as to the need to understand the interrelatedness of and the dynamic movements among the FS. For Lonergan, *MiT*, 268, theology is ordered by "a fully conscious decision in foundations about one's horizon . . ., one's worldview. It deliberately selects the framework, in which doctrines have their meaning, in which systematics reconciles, in which communications are effective." An analogous process occurs when addressing issues such as healthcare.

8. Lonergan, "Belief: Today's Issue," 87.

Significant scientific and medical judgments made by some are not at first generally accepted by all—they are considered as merely probable. From a GEM-FS viewpoint, scientific conclusions are the best available opinion of the time. Lonergan revolutionizes the practice of scientific research from being an object-oriented effort to a subject-based heuristic endeavor.[9] In spelling out the vectors of human history and progress, Lonergan analyzes the development of the modern sciences as a primary example of self-transcending human consciousness. One moves from attentiveness to experience to refined understanding to critical judgments. In *Insight*, he probes this process in the development of mathematics and the natural sciences. This leads to his overall view of world processes as emergent probability which he links with finality. Emergent probability is a factor in human affairs as well as in the world of nature. Both of these are open dynamic processes.[10]

Lonergan stresses the need for intellectual conversion in order to correctly understand science and link the various sciences to one another. The fact is, however, that human biases militate against the smooth functioning of human intelligence—this leads to moral failures. The biases provoke decline. Lonergan's cognitional analysis sheds light on this dilemma, as Daly realizes. Lonergan tackles such issues by analyzing contemporary scientific methods in the light of emergent probability. Integral and closely related to Lonergan's analysis of consciousness as deriving from a moral "ought" is the imperative of assessing the facts of a situation. Note that when operating under a static model, people tend to repeat the same actions over and over again, but through the directives of a dynamic self-corrective GEM-FS process method, progress toward goals can occur. This may shed light on the exigencies and processes underlying Lonergan's move toward the second mediated-healing phase in *MiT*.

---

9. This is due to Lonergan's grasp of history and faith-commitment which enables his GEM-FS to appeal to healing-creating vectors in history whereby one can deploy the heuristic structures used in many human endeavors.

10. Lonergan, *Insight*, 470–76. "The essential meaning of finality is that it goes beyond" the determinations of "some determinate individual or species or genus of proportionate being." Here are involved interplays between potency, form, and act since potency leads not only to form but also to act. "It heads beyond act to coincidental manifolds of acts, and through them to higher forms and higher coincident manifolds of acts," etc. (Lonergan, *Insight*, 473).

Moving from the First Mediating-Creative Phase to the Second Mediated-Healing Phase in *MiT*'s Self-Transcending Process Method

In *MiT*'s FS 5, Lonergan moves into the mediated-healing phase. He transposes, expands upon his definition of a basic set of terms and relations characterizing a person's conscious knowing-doing operations given in *Insight* to include those of interiority, life of prayer, etc.[11] This expanded notion can promote and facilitate collaboration and promote societal healing. Such a multi-tasking includes addressing how a secularist stance differs from a religious one. While FS 4, dialectic, focuses on ways to buttress one's own view, FS 5 would promote ideal types that do not remain in a Platonic realm. Rather, they are to be applied in a diphase GEM-FS feedback process to facilitate human cooperation. Let us recall how the great pioneers Mendel and Pasteur were sustained by their faith, their sense of values. Or we might advert to the example of Rudolf Carl Virchow (1821–1912), known as the founder of modern medicine. Virchow was also an anthropologist, a prehistorian, a biologist. He promoted clinical observation, animal experimentation to determine causes of diseases and the effects of drugs. He pioneered the modern concept of pathological processes due to his application of the cell theory. He emphasized that diseases arose primarily in individual cells of the tissues. He is considered as one of the founders of social medicine who campaigned vigorously for social reforms and contributed to the development of anthropology as a modern science. Obviously, such great pioneers and their steadfast convictions testify to the authentic foundations that Lonergan generalizes in FS 5.

Foundations is the pivot of a diphase GEM-FS process based on self-appropriation through the several conversions. As the basic operations are verifiable on experiential levels (in perceiving and imagining), on the intellectual levels (of understanding, formulating concepts, weighing the evidence and in judging and acting), so FS 5 initiates one into the processes of the mediated phase. The question is to what extent has Daly adverted to and explored this critical GEM-FS function? I am trying to situate his model within a larger GEM-FS perspective by insisting on the need to situate Lonergan's authentic foundations as grounded in love. Many, not to say the majority of people today, are driven by secular "values." This leads them and even authoritative voices to overlook the needed and stable foundations grounded in love that are needed in our rapidly changing,

---

11. Michael Shute, *Origins*, argues that Lonergan began using "affective self-transcendence" in his post-*Method* writings applying it to religious self-transcendence and conversion.

technology-driven, secular world.¹² Daly does not overlook this dimension but he fails to make it *explicitly foundational* in *mediated-healing* ways.

Much of what we believed to be true twenty or thirty years ago has been shown to be incorrect or in need of modification as new clinical research studies have provided new evidence, deeper insights. Although the foundation for clinical practice is based on clinical training and experience, clinical practice guidelines and a continual review of newly published articles in the medical literature form the basis upon which many physicians modify or improve their clinical practice. Physicians rely on the recommendations made by clinical practice guidelines, assuming that they are based on the best evidence that is available for the effective diagnosis and management of a specific condition.¹³ My interest here is to do full justice to Lonergan's overall legacy by not shortchanging its real foundation. This foundation is crucial, for example, in FS 7's goal to develop adequate policies for healthcare.¹⁴ The GEM-FS diphase process allows persons and even disciplines to cooperate to the extent people appropriate their inbuilt bridge's basic structure which, in turn, could enable them to erect transcultural bridges, for example.¹⁵

---

12. For Lonergan, "Dialectic of Authority," 9, to fall in love is "to set up a new principle that has, indeed, its causes, conditions, occasions, but, as long as it lasts, provides the mainspring of one's desire and fear, hope and despair, joy and sorrow. In the measure that the community becomes a community of love and so capable of making real and great sacrifices, in that measure it can wipe out the grievances and correct the objective absurdities unauthenticity has brought about."

13. Harrison et al., "Addressing," 54, argue that "The goal of clinical practice guidelines is to reduce unwarranted variation in care, thereby leading to consistent, efficient, and high-quality care."

14. The GEM-FS diphase process allows persons and even disciplines to cooperate if and when people have appropriated their inbuilt bridge's basic structure, enabling them to erect transcultural bridges

15. See Raymaker, *Empowering Bernard Lonergan's Legacy*, which uses GEM-FS process matrices to this effect. There, I also argue that eight-step FS process, grounded in feedback, can uplift our hearts so as to build more just societies. GEM's synergetic matrices could globally enable interfaith, ethical, and transcultural actions, based on an ethics of social responsibility in our world. It could do so by integrating disciplines through the operational invariance of each one's inbuilt, feedback cognitive structure that Lonergan first developed in *Insight* and then systematically explained in *MiT*'s eight FS-feedback-process.

Healing and Creating in History—Hints to Lonergan's Grand Foundational Strategy

In "Healing and Creating in History,"[16] Lonergan notes that our four basic operations are "creative vectors" to the extent that we correct our biases and confront evil. Some describe human-historical existence in negative terms. William James described it positively, underpinned by one's fluent world of consciousness.[17] Citing James's notion of the three stages in a theory's "career," Lonergan shares an insight into his own lifework. A new theory is first rejected, then admitted as true but obvious; "finally it is seen to be so important that its adversaries"[18] claim credit for it. GEM *creates* from below upwards and *heals* from above downwards—hence my reliance on GEM-FS's mediating-creative and mediated-healing phases. In "Healing-Creating," Lonergan agrees with both Bertrand Russell who says that humanity is too clever and wicked for its own good and with Karl Popper's claim[19] that humanity's moral enthusiasm is misplaced. While Christianity healed the Roman Empire's ills, it failed to *create* so that the Dark Ages ensued.[20] The creating-healing vectors complement one another. They help integrate the reason-and-faith aspects of our lives. We need a creative process, a grand strategy that unfolds in an orderly and cumulative series of steps. In some respects, GEM-FS parallels Gregory Bateson's view that the unconscious algorithms of the heart transcend those of language.[21] Since much of conscious thought "is structured in terms of the logics of language, the algorithms of the unconscious are doubly inaccessible. . . . The operations of the unconscious are structured in terms of *primary process*" characterized as "lacking negatives and/or any linguistic mood. The discourse of primary process is metaphorical."[22]

---

16. Lonergan, "Healing and Creating in History," 100–109.
17. James, *Principles*, 239.
18. Lonergan, "Healing and Creating in History," 102; see also 109.
19. GEM-FS nuances Lakatos's *Methodology* which vacillates between Popper and the Duhem–Quine thesis that holds that it is impossible to test a scientific hypothesis in isolation since an empirical test of the hypothesis requires one or more background assumptions.
20. Lonergan, "Healing and Creating in History," 107.
21. Bateson, *Steps*, 139.
22. Bateson, *Steps*, 139. For Oyler, "Philosophy," the FS, as associated with different general contexts of operations (levels), are metaphorical in the sense that there is a correlation between the results of the full set of operations for each specialization in each field and the context of consciousness that provides the potentiality for the field of its achievement. The relation between the general contexts of FS and the operations is analogical, not metaphorical; but if the relation is thought of in terms of levels, then it

Linking GEM-FS Psychic Processes within Evolutionary Processes[23]

One has to adequately grasp how primary process and the intermediate zone that lies between it and secondary process work in *Insight* taken as a set of exercises in intellectual therapy (or could work, e.g., in the study of the world religions to establish parameters for a global spirituality). For Robert Doran, the primary processes, directly animated by the drives, serve the pleasure principle and work to actualize a free flow of psychic energy. Secondary processes, which presuppose the binding of this energy, intervene as a system of control and regulation in the service of the reality principle.[24] Endorsed by Lonergan, Doran's contribution involves transposing the notion of "passionateness of being" into the category of interiorly differentiated consciousness of *psychic conversion* as being implicit in Lonergan's work. Lonergan describes it as a "deeper and more comprehensive principle . . . a tidal movement that begins before consciousness, unfolds through sensitivity, intelligence, rational reflection, responsible deliberation, only to find its rest beyond all of these."[25]

While Lonergan acknowledges this psychic dimension as a separate dimension that accompanies intentionality, he does not clearly identify "levels" in the psychic dimension. He did begin to venture into such notions by referring to a "quasi-operator" and a "topmost quasi-operator"—terms that Doran uses 1) to distinguish three separate "levels" in the psyche and their corresponding aesthetic-dramatic operators that "underpin, accompany, and overarch"[26] intentionality, and 2) to expand his notion of

---

is metaphorical. Among Anglo-Saxons, it is rather usual to think of the "reasons" of the heart or of the unconscious as inchoate forces or pushes—what Freud called *Trieben*. To Pascal, for whom the heart has its reasons which reason fails to perceive, the matter was different. Pascal no doubt thought of the heart's reasons as a body of logic as precise and complex as those of consciousness. See "Primary Process."

23. I am considering GEM-FS in its full amplitude as a dialectical-foundational process based on our basic operations. For the noted American biologist, Edward O. Wilson, "we have Paleolithic emotions, medieval institutions and godlike technology." (During a debate at the Harvard Museum of Natural History, 9 September 2009). GEM-FS process is designed to reach a larger consensus due to its ability to get beyond our paleolithic emotions, such as fear, jealousy, and greed. Indeed, our ability to manipulate RNA and DNA, bacteria, viruses, algae and fungi gives us the power to engineer life.

24. See Doran, *Subject and Psyche*. For Doran, psychic conversion is part of a single process of human transformation promoting human development. McDonald, "Body-Psyche-Mind," focuses on Doran's notion of the "passionateness of being" in categories of interiority as being a dimension of intentional consciousness.

25. Lonergan, "Natural Right," 175.

26. See Dunne, "Being in Love," 161–75.

psychic conversion to include the self-appropriation of all three levels of the psychic dimension in their correspondence to intentionality.

In showing God's compassionate love present in all of life's stages, GEM-FS's transformative process method presupposes forms of commitment (foundational conversions) on the part of those who would cooperate in living God's love.[27] Daly seems to take for granted the forms of personal commitment that Lonergan insists on as the foundational reality needed to transcend one's previous horizon. It is important to make explicit the intellectual and religious foundations that Daly only partly adverts to.[28] This must be spelled out on the lines of *MiT*'s second mediated-healing phase so as to realize more fully the hopes Daly places in GEM.[29] The spelling out can, in turn, provide a deeper appreciation of the work done by medical personnel involved, for example, in Doctors without Borders. It may also help motivate more persons to participate in the outreach of the World Health Organization. Both of these organizations provide a global context to evaluate and address the lamentable tragedies that have provoked countless instances of man's inhumanity to man across the globe.

Tackling Some Dark, Disturbing Injustices in the World Manifested in COVID-19 Events—Doing So in Both One's Daily and Professional Life

In a May 5, 2020 message, Jim Simpson, a writer for *Sojourners,* alerted its readers to the fact that the COVID-19 pandemic has accented the dark and disturbing injustices and inequities that have always existed in health care and the economy, and still occur even in many governmental policies:

> Though the virus may not discriminate, our human-made systems and structures do. And in the United States this means that those who are feeling the impact of this disease most acutely are

---

27. The Buddha had an inkling of this, but formed his insights into compassion in a form of "unknowing" that leads to detachment. On the other side of the coin, one must face the reality outlined in a private exchange by Mike Dempsey, a change management consultant in a psychiatric hospital in California, namely, that one cannot but conclude that the current medical model of psychiatric care (based on medication management) "is grossly materialistic, reducing the soul (psyche) to so many neural clusters. It is a dehumanizing model."

28. Lonergan, *MiT*, 267.

29. In "Healing and Creating," Lonergan highlights people's creative movements from below within their own consciousness—but also the radically-healing movements from above as outlined in Fig. 1.

those who have been historically, structurally, systemically, and politically marginalized and oppressed.

In revealing these injustices, the COVID-19 pandemic should cause us to reflect individually and collectively on the brokenness of our society and world and to commit, with renewed vigor, to addressing these injustices . . .

Globally, this is both a health crisis and an economic crisis. In the United States, we face an additional reality that, because of our deeply broken health care system, a health crisis *is* already an economic crisis for many people in America.[30]

Simpson in *Sojourners* concluded that "As we move deeper into this health crisis, the economic impacts are being felt by more and more people. Millions of people are performing essential work and millions more are people for whom work is essential."[31] However, millions of others saw themselves caught up in the catch-twenty-two of wanting to maintain their physical health without going into debt. The spread of the COVID-19 virus gave rise to disinformation about its origin, diffusion, and effects. Some ill-intentioned people exploited the great speed of news propagation on digital platforms. Given the large number of incorrect statements on the Internet, it became very difficult to limit their circulation because fact-checking takes much time and effort. People died from taking drugs passed off as useful. The information verification process on diseases has been in trouble for some time. The pandemic has made the problem plain for all to see.

In the latter part of 2020, the ramifications of COVID-19 were exacerbated by flooding, wildfires, hurricanes, and heatwaves. The Federal Emergency Management Agency, already stretched thin providing response and recovery to help communities around the country, was further strained from compounding extreme weather events.[32] In the face of such realities, how might one assess the importance of *transitioning* from the first creative phase of GEM-FS process to the second healing phase on which Lonergan insists? Lonergan has explained how and why the subject as subject is GEM-FS' foundational[33] reality. This is why I seek to transpose Daly's GEM model

30. Simpson, "Normal Wasn't Working," paras. 1–3.

31. Simpson, "Normal Wasn't Working," para. 3.

32. See the website for the Union of Concerned Scientists at ucsusa.org. We should be ever grateful to the dedicated persons, public servants, and/or communal organizers who seek the good throughout the globe. This would include the family-community aspects of medicine, the contributions of religious orders in the missions, and many dedicated scientists.

33. Lonergan's method helps us integrate revolutionary efforts within various traditions while opening up paths to interfaith, interdisciplinary perspectives. His work offers us several dialectical-foundational missing links that can help connect the

into a more encompassing GEM-FS-process approach. Daly has prepared a way upon which to build. GEM-FS can draw out some of the foundational implications of Daly's first-phase approach to Lonergan's achievement. But there is a need for fuller cooperation in organized, spiritually-morally-motivated ways. For example, how can we best help motivate young nursing and medical students to serve others rather than being "in it for the money"?

Doctors without Borders exemplify self-transcendence in their altruistic dedication to global needs. *MiT*'s foundational stance can lay seeds for such self-transcending dedication. God has entered history with the gift of his love. Christians accept this initiative from God through faith—the eye of love. It is this eye that enables some humans to act heroically in times of difficulty (think of Saint Peter Claver, who ministered to slaves; Damien the Leper; or Mother Teresa). In more pedestrian ways, an eye of love enriches one's daily life for it is a "mystical eye" that penetrates below the surface of life's sordid aspects so as to react with selfless love. Faith is an embryonic mystical experience; it lets one transcend adversities. One recognizes it when it happens. (See Appendix D.)

In practice, it is not easy to apply Lonergan's method in everyday life—especially if it is interpreted only as a "model." One must reach further and deeper. In *MiT* and some of his other writings, Lonergan reminds us that Christianity urges us to live loving lives which is *a self-transcending process*. To adapt Lonergan's method to such a vision, we need intermediate thinkers such as Daly, who rightly focuses on implementing method in such a critical field as medicine. Daly's various articles are good efforts toward relating to health care theory and practice. His GEM model takes on a special relevance given the present global pandemic—even though his articles were written before the outbreak. But a mere GEM model, though relevant for health care because it includes an account of the human good and seeks to anchor itself in spiritual realities as provided in Lonergan's method, overlooks or minimizes GEM-FS's key feedback process dimensions.

---

intellectual and spiritual facets of our lives both personally in multicultural endeavors. But opposed to this optimistic prognosis for Lonergan's method, the effectiveness of his achievement is undermined by what Phil McShane in "Positive Anthropocene" calls the "darkness" affecting humans—a darkness that has not spared the efforts of Lonergan students. "That darkness gives us the possibility, even some slim probabilities, of a fresh start on the stumbling meaning of *Method in Theology* from Section 5 of chapter ten to the end of the book. That stumbling meaning has to become a precise lean-forward meaning" hinted at in *Method in Theology*'s chapter on history. McShane, "Positive Anthropocene," para. 2.

Postulating a mRNA-Conversion Analogue

As to overlooking this key GEM-FS role, one may cite the astonishing feat of how researchers were able to create a vaccine against COVID-19 in record time made possible due to years of research based on how mRNA works within our bodies.[34] Traditionally, making vaccines required growing viruses in giant vats of cells. The mRNA approach is radically different. It starts with a snippet of genetic code that carries instructions for making proteins and then helps the body target the virus. It turns the body itself into a miniature vaccine factory. More than does Daly's one-phase model, GEM-FS diphase process accentuates the roles of the conversions in combatting evil and the biases.[35] In my view, the conversions are an analogue to how mRNA works in the body to ward off threats. Ideally, they could help fulfill Daly's wish to motivate patients and healthcare providers. Daly does stress that religion and spiritual beliefs play important roles for many patients. When illness threatens the health or even the life of a patient, he or she is likely to come to the physician with both physical symptoms and spiritual issues in mind. Daly notes how friendship may contribute to our health and well-being and that values are not to be conceived as mere instrumental notions. These are inherently good. This is a claim that can be quite perplexing unless one recognizes the realm of transcendence. Daly argues that dominant models of health care tend to overlook this issue, but that his GEM model does address it in realistic ways. His model assesses human historical decline and real need for creative and healing trends in human history. It seeks to restore and maintain healthy functioning of well-established schemes and to give answers to new, disturbing questions about

---

34. In molecular biology, mRNA is a single-stranded molecule of RNA that corresponds to the genetic sequence of a gene, and is read by a ribosome in the process of synthesizing a protein. Transcription is the process of copying a gene from the DNA into mRNA. In hindsight, I argue that in *MiT*'s second phase, Lonergan developed a method to combat the "pandemic" of the biases, evils, and false philosophical presuppositions haunting human life. The second phase's conversions can be taken as an analogue of how mRNA functions in targeting the COVID-19 virus.

35. GEM-FS is relevant to the study of all sciences, the humanities, and in interreligious dialogue-cooperation. GEM is the general method, whereas a scientific method such as relativity is a special method. One extrapolates into the "isomorphism" of ethical/moral reflection as does Lonergan in *Insight* and in his section on "Value" in *MiT*, 34–41. McShane, *Futurology*, notes that it is a difficult climb for either the physicists or the philosophers to get to grips with the cycle of FS collaboration as being essential to all human inquiry. All scientific method must move into this zone in the next century or so. The issues raised in *Insight* and in *MiT* on the human good and values can only be met effectively in the full diphase GEM-FS cyclical structure and its processes of verification.

what we can do both individually and collectively "in our personal struggles to forge or develop meaningful narratives for our lives, or as in our collective efforts to develop an effective explanatory dimension in collaborative education for social change."[36] These are laudable goals for medicine. But a GEM-FS transformative process method reaches deeper as suggested in my mRNA-conversion analogue which I invoke to help draw out GEM-FS's full implications and possibilities in tackling our biases and moral failings.

Ironically, Daly partially begs the question as to how his GEM model can make a difference in improving or reforming health care. For Lonergan, there is needed in such an endeavor a thorough exploration of *MiT* s second *healing* phase, beginning with FS 5. Daly stresses that his GEM model involves much more than simple judgments of fact for it probes integral values deeply, recognizing, for instance, how scientists or any serious thinker must through the values embedded in various sets of acquired beliefs, rely on others' judgments for their knowledge. This "entails decisions of trust and acceptance of another's testimony in judgments of fact. Belief then is an integral and often assumed part of any science as are the judgments of value associated with trusting others in any serious field of practice or tradition."[37] This is indeed an important point that Daly makes here, but it has to be further elaborated. One should show how *MiT* grounds divisive beliefs within the deeper aspects of faith.[38] The deeper roots of faith would shed more light on Daly's own laudable project which does suggest many practical facets such as how values can or should function in daily life. In our secularized age this is a critical point. In *MiT*, Lonergan specifies that instilling values in a secularized society involves the role of the categories. His *Insight* does not explore the role and importance of the categories in great depth other than by commenting on their roles in Aristotle and Kant—though it does speak of "category as psychogenic" in depth psychology.[39] Insights are part "of a therapeutic process that ends with an illuminating moment in which

---

36. Daly, "GEM Model," 421.

37. Daly, "GEM Model," 421.

38. Lonergan, *MiT*, 115–17, appeals to W. Cantwell Smith's distinction between faith and beliefs. He writes that "faith is the knowledge born of religious love. . . . Without faith, without the eye of love, the world is too evil for God to be good. He notes that "faith and progress have a common root in in man's cognitional and moral self-transcendence." Beliefs, on the other hand, are peculiar to various religions' ways of expressing their creeds. They are often divisive, as witnessed by the various conflicting interpretations that Christians and Muslims have of their respective scriptures.

39. Lonergan, *Insight*, 227–31.

previous thinking falls into perspective and sensitive spontaneity undergoes an effortless change."[40]

To further draw out the full implications of the categories in Lonergan's work, one must turn to his treatment of them in FS 5 where he distinguishes between special categories which are particular to theology and general categories. There exist bases for deriving these two types of categories which "in some measure . . . are transcultural."[41] As to the validity of the derivation, Lonergan writes that

> the explicit formulation of [his transcendental] method is historically conditioned and can be expected to be corrected, modified, complemented as the sciences continue to advance and reflection on them to improve. What is transcultural is the reality to which such formulation refers, and that reality is transcultural because it is not the product of any culture but rather the principle that begets and develops cultures that flourish, as it is also the principle that is violated when cultures crumble and decay.[42]

Lonergan then makes a distinction as to the base of special theological categories. The distinction touches on whether one is

> in love in an unrestricted manner (1) as it is defined and (2) as it is achieved. As it is defined, it is the habitual actuation of mans' capacity for self-transcendence; it is the religious conversion that grounds both moral and intellectual conversion; it provides the real criterion by which all else is to be judged; and consequently one has only to experience it in oneself or witness it in others to find in it its own justification. On the other hand, as it actually is achieved in any human being, the achievement is dialectical. It is authenticity as a withdrawal from inauthenticity, and the withdrawal is never complete and always precarious.[43]

Here we may refer to how in 1978, Lonergan, writing on the topic of authenticity and inauthenticity, notes that an existential decision attains substance and moment in the measure that it transforms one's conduct and pursuits. He defines levels of integration using the mathematical analogue of "operators" and the existence of a symbolic operator (unrestricted loving) that may remind us of Kierkegaard. "This would be a distinct operator

---

40. Lonergan, *Insight*, 227.
41. Lonergan, *MiT*, 283.
42. Lonergan, *MiT*, 283.
43. Lonergan, *MiT*, 284.

beyond that of the moral operator."[44] The principle that Lonergan invokes here is that of transforming or "sublating"[45] the operations within one's worldview or horizon. Just as in symbolic consciousness we reach the "border" of our usual conscious intentionality from below, so in religious consciousness we reach the "border" of our conscious intentionality from above. Both borders surround consciousness with transforming mystery. Genuine symbolic consciousness is an orientation from the unconscious to transcendence. The experience of transcendence reorients symbolic consciousness. Psychic vitality energizes the levels of conscious intentionality; spiritual luminosity alters the very horizon of experience, understanding, judging, and deciding.[46] Again using the mRNA analogy, the spiritual reorientation of symbolic consciousness corresponds to how the body becomes its own producer of defenses against an invading virus; it also helps underpin the crucial way of transitioning from FS 5 to FS 6.

The Crucial Way of Transitioning from FS 5 to FS 6 and Lonergan's Use of Models

Noting that the basic nest of terms and relations of GEM-FS process can be differentiated in a number of ways as they apply to individual persons or to persons in groups, Lonergan writes:

> With regard to transcendental method and with regard to God's gift of his love we have distinguished between an inner core, which is transcultural, and an outer manifestation that is subject to variation.... Theological categories will be transcultural only insofar as they refer to that inner core. In their actual formulation they will be historically conditioned.[47]

---

44. Lonergan, "Philosophy and the Religious Phenomenon," 400, acknowledges his debt to Robert Doran for his notion of symbolic operator.

45. Lonergan, *MiT*, 241, writes that he uses the notion of sublation in "Karl Rahner's sense rather than Hegel's to mean that what sublates goes beyond what is sublated, introduces something new and distinct, puts everything on a new basis, yet so far from interfering with the sublated or destroying it, on the contrary needs it, includes it, preserves all its proper feature and properties, and carries them forward to a fuller realization within a richer context." Lonergan adds that "moral conversion goes beyond the value of truth, to values generally."

46. See McPartland, "Religious Phenomenon," 125. On Lonergan's study of the development of Aquinas's views on grace and how these anticipate the main points of *MiT*'s mediated phase, see Appendix A.

47. Lonergan, *MiT*, 284.

Importantly, it is at this critical junction that Lonergan introduces "the notion of the model or ideal-type" on which Daly relies but which I argue Lonergan himself transcends with the more encompassing reality of GEM-FS process he outlines in *MiT*.[48] Lonergan comments on his use of models to the effect that when one possesses models, the task of framing a hypothesis is reduced to the simpler matter of tailoring a model to suit a given object or area. Moreover, "the utility of the model may arise when it comes to describing a known reality. For known realities can be exceedingly complicated, and an adequate language to describe them hard to come by."[49]

Lonergan concludes that it is up to the theologian (or in our case up to the healthcare commentator) "to decide whether any model is to become an hypothesis or to be taken as a description." I am arguing that a GEM-FS process approach is more basic; it transcends mere hypotheses, models or descriptions. While models in general and Daly's use of a GEM model to characterize Lonergan's method are helpful, the inherent process of a *generalized* empirical method *functionally specialized* (GEM-FS) gets to the core of Lonergan's achievement in *Insight* and in *MiT*. Lonergan, himself, in *Insight*'s section, "Method in Metaphysics," writes "A method is a set of directives that serve to guide a process towards a result"[50] After noting that "bluntly, the starting point of metaphysics is people as they are," he adds,

> Between this starting point and the goal, there is the process. It is a process from latent to explicit metaphysics. . . . The process then, to explicit metaphysics is primarily a process to self-knowledge. . . . Since an appeal to disorientated knowledge would only extend and confirm the disorientation, the appeal must be to the desire that is prior to knowledge, that generates knowledge, that can effect the correction of miscarriages in the cognitional process.[51]

---

48. Lonergan grants that the formulation of models helps us describe and communicate a known reality, but both in *MiT*'s treatment of the heuristic structures used by historians (229), and in "Foundations" (285), Lonergan speaks of the enormous complexities that ideal-types or models "never grasp" in their full complexity (229). I argue that it is not merely a matter of using a model as a helpful tool; rather, it involves the *process* of deciding "whether any model is to become an hypothesis or to be taken as description" (285). A crucial point is whether models are built up from basic terms and relations that refer to transcultural components in human living and operational procedures and whether they are subject to structural processes "within which the operations occur" (286).

49. Lonergan, *MiT*, 285.

50. Lonergan, *Insight*, 421.

51. Lonergan, *Insight*, 422.

I rely on this notion of transformative process in my whole text and particularly in moving from FS 5 foundations to FS 6 on "implementing adequate policies."

SIXTH FUNCTIONAL SPECIALTY: POLICIES FOR IMPLEMENTING HEALTH CARE TODAY[52]

As to addressing how to implement health care today, Lonergan's treatment of doctrines (FS 6) and systematics (FS 7) in *MiT* gives us a template for doing so. The template I wish to address revolves around a notion of recycling institutional policies that result in new systems. In fact, policy developments and system changes are closely related partly due to the reduplicative feedback inherent in GEM-FS process. Lonergan himself suggests the close link between FS 6 and FS 7 when he writes: "The seventh functional specialty, systematics, is concerned with promoting an understanding of the realities affirmed in the previous specialty, doctrines."[53] In our case, I argue that the policies which institutions develop are inevitably related to the type of systems they use to implement their policies. As to why this is so, we may briefly consider Daly's stress on how Lonergan's account of higher viewpoints provides an ontological basis for both the differentiation and integration of the generic levels of human living.

Daly stresses Lonergan's argument in *Insight* that in a universe in which the same things have properties investigated in distinct, autonomous sciences, *the notion of successive higher viewpoints is alone* capable of "intelligibly relating the generically distinct properties of the same thing without violating the autonomy of the sciences."[54] This point, Daly writes, is key to

---

52. A question is whether the policies of medical groups (including those of the World Health Organization) and also those of individual medical practitioners are adequate. "Healing and Creating" implicitly addresses such a question.

53. Lonergan, *MiT*, 335.

54. Lonergan, *Insight*, 510. He adds. "There follows a generalized emergent probability for both things and events, and the heuristic structure of knowing is matched by the finality of being." The physicist Michael Bretz, "Emergent Probability," evaluates Lonergan's view of emergent probability as "an early model of complexity, . . . a cohesive body of explanatory knowledge as a convoluted building process of *recurrent schemes* (RS) that act as foundational elements to further growth" (1; italics original). Bretz refers to other examples of recurrent growth as schemes that "abound in nature: resource cycles, motor skills, biological routines, autocatalytic processes, etc. The corresponding growing generic *World Process* can alternatively be thought of as chemical, environmental, evolutionary, social, organizational, economical, psychological, or ethical . . . and its generality might be of particular interest to complex systems researchers" (1; italics original). RS "are conjoined dynamic activities where, in simplest form, each

understanding his GEM model of health. Yet, he pays little attention to the differentiations of consciousness that Lonergan stresses as a key *MiT* theme. In fact, such differentiations are needed to buttress Daly's GEM model. That this is so can be discerned, for example, in the way Lonergan transitions in *MiT* from FS 5 (foundations) to FS 6 (doctrines). In the latter, referring to the development of doctrines, Lonergan speaks of the logical and metaphysical contexts within which doctrines evolved in the church:

> The fully metaphysical context emerges only in a late and full self-conscious Scholasticism. But in its fundamental intention and style Scholasticism was a thorough-going effort to attain a coherent and orderly assimilation of the Christian tradition. The enormous differences between the two great figures, Anselm of Canterbury and Thomas Aquinas, were the result of a century and a half of unremitting labors to assemble and classify the data, to work towards an understanding of them in commentaries, to digest them by establishing the existence of questions and by seeking solutions for them, and to ensure the coherence of multitudinous solutions by using the Aristotelian corpus as a substructure.[55]

In 1979, Lonergan answered an objection that there is "no logical connection" between his position and that of Aquinas. He stressed that he was not talking about a conclusion but a transposition of horizons. He pointed to his "own intellectual therapy" which had advanced after writing *Insight* when he began to distinguish *a series of horizontal and vertical processes*:

> Each horizontal process has its own principle, yielding moments, first of movement and then of rest, on the successive levels of sensitivity, intelligence, reasonableness, and responsibility. The vertical process springs from an undifferentiated *eros*, commonly referred as the unconscious, influences in turn each of the horizontal movements, and finds its proper goal beyond them in a self-transcending being-in-love that begins in the home, reaches out to the tribe, the city-state, the nation,

---

element generates the next action, which in turn generates the next, until the last dynamic regenerates the first one again, locking the whole scheme into long term stable equilibrium. BL [Bernard Lonergan] modeled generic growth as the successive appearance of conditioned *Recurrent Schemes* (RS), each of which comes into function with high probabilistically once all required prior schemes have become functional. RS's can be treated as dynamic black cells of activity which themselves may contain internal structures and dynamic schemes of arbitrary complexity" (1; italics original).

55. Lonergan, *MiT*, 309.

mankind, and finds its anchor and its strength in the agape of the New Testament.[56]

Lonergan then traces the history of European thought, the emergence of method in Europe that began with Abelard in the twelfth century as these have been impacted, for instance, by the emergence of secularism and the response of Vatican II to such developments. He contrasts the philosophical approaches of Aquinas and Kant on the relation between philosophy and theology. Unlike Aquinas, Kant separated philosophy from theology which in fact influenced the advance of a secularized West.[57] Having analyzed such developments, Lonergan turns to address "The New Notion of Science" and how his process method is "critical in the sense that its terms and relations have their empirical counterpart in the experienced terms and experienced relations of cognitional theory.[58] The themes of science today and of policies for implementing healthcare today can, of course, no longer be addressed with the principles of Aristotle's *Posterior Analytics* echoed by Aquinas. "In fact, modern science is concerned mainly, not with the intelligibility of the necessary but with the intelligibility of the possible."[59] Commenting on this, Daly stresses that science and medicine today are very much concerned with accurately addressing concrete situations. He refers to Lonergan's argument that the sciences reserve "a notable role for statistical laws, which speak simply of concrete events that are likely to occur."[60] He cautions lest in the face of the great stress on statistics, some physicians succumb to the tendency to change the focus of medicine from a caring, service-oriented model to a technological, cure-oriented one.

---

56. Lonergan, "Horizons and Transpositions," 413. Disciplines only function correctly when guided by persons grounded in a basic horizon. GEM-FS details a precise opposition between self-transcendence and the self as transcended—one that involves a self-corrective process of knowing-doing. Here the analogy between circulatory-vascular systems and GEM-FS functioning in Fig. 1 can be applied. The rub is how can "converted" persons function so as to overcome the biases and overcome the disorganizations of human life. Here Lonergan's notions of differentiated consciousness, of development and of higher viewpoints can help.

57. Lonergan, "Horizons and Transpositions," 427.

58. Lonergan, "Horizons and Transpositions," 429.

59. Lonergan, "Horizons and Transpositions," 429.

60. Lonergan, "Horizons and Transpositions," 429.

On Not Over-Emphasizing Technology at the Expense of the Spiritual

On this theme, let me cite two efforts by American researchers who have also reacted against an overemphasis on technological models in medicine. First, Rachel Remen, MD, organizer of Commonweal Retreats for People with Cancer, writes:

> Technology has led to phenomenal advances in medicine and has given us the ability to prolong life. However, in the past few decades physicians have attempted to balance their care by reclaiming medicine's more spiritual roots, recognizing that until modern times spirituality was often linked with health care. Spiritual or compassionate care involves serving the whole person—the physical, emotional, social, and spiritual.[61]

Secondly, Lisa Rose-Wiles has reported on a Seton Hall University Workshop (2017) that examined how Lonergan's FS can be applied to medicine—the premise being that the FS provide a language for interdisciplinary conversation:

> We wanted to share what we had achieved (being) eager for feedback, including constructive criticism. When we began preparing for this workshop, we were frankly intimidated. Our Praxis participants are not Lonergan scholars. They 'apply Lonergan' to the best of their abilities, without extensive (or in some cases, any) background in theology, philosophy or Lonergan's work beyond that which we have studied together as part of the Praxis Program.[62]

For his part, Daly, in pleading for sound medical policies, recalls that serving patients may involve spending time with them, holding their hands, and talking about what is important to them. He discusses elements of compassionate care, of the role of spirituality in health care, and he highlights the advantages of understanding patients' spirituality. He summarizes some

---

61. Pulchalski, "Role," 352. Rachel Remen adds: "Helping, fixing, and serving represent three different ways of seeing life. When you help, you see life as weak. When you fix, you see life as broken. When you serve, you see life as whole. Fixing and helping may be the work of the ego, and service the work of the soul." Remen, "Helping, Fixing, or Serving?," 1.

62. Rose-Wiles stresses that Lonergan's study of theoretical and practical reason, as a problem-solving process in *Insight*, is relevant to questions of medical practice. *MiT*'s functional specialties provide a framework. See Rose-Wiles, "Functional Specialties."

national efforts to incorporate spirituality into medicine,[63] a policy suggestion that brings us to the seventh functional specialty and the need to address possible systemic shortcomings in healthcare.

SEVENTH FUNCTIONAL SPECIALTY: DEALING WITH SYSTEMIC SHORTCOMINGS IN HEALTHCARE

Daly makes several important comments on the roles of systematics in Lonergan's overall thinking. He notes that Lonergan has stressed that "Data must either conform or not conform to system, and successive systems must be either related or not related in a directly intelligible manner."[64] He adds that

> Classical method seeks to understand data in terms of their constant systematic interrelations; for instance, classical mechanics. Genetic method seeks to understand data in terms of an intelligibly related sequence of systematic interrelations; for instance, developmental biology. Statistical method seeks to understand the extent to which data do not conform to constant system; for instance, quantum mechanics and epidemiology. Dialectical method seeks to understand data regarding the relations between successive stages of a changing system that are not directly intelligible; for instance, political science. Despite the anticipated generality of the systems and structures toward which they head, these methods rely on data that are all individual—for discovery, verification, and application. Insights regarding concrete unities are needed in addition to insights regarding structural interrelations in order to link individual data with general structures. In addition to being unified by concrete reference to individual data, these methods are also unified structurally in complementing one another with respect to investigating world order—emergent probability—and in virtue of relating what we learn from distinct, autonomous sciences in terms of successive higher viewpoints.[65]

1. Daly commendably argues that it is problematic that the dominant models for health care tend to overlook the systematic difference between nature and history, between pre-intentional levels of biological

---

63. Daly, "Integral Approach to Health Science," 15.
64. Lonergan, *Insight*, 509–10.
65. Daly, "Model of Health," 431. Lonergan, *Reader*, 252–53 specifies that genetic method is concerned with a sequence of operators that successively generate further functions from an initial function.

functioning and the intentional levels of psycho-social functioning, and further, that there have been insufficient attempts to integrate the humanities into these models where they would interact and collaborate with the natural and human sciences in probing much deeper questions concerning the human prospect, or the human good. There have been some proposals for adding or combining psycho-cognitive elements so that there can be treatment of patients/clients at the psychological, cognitive, emotional, and social levels of functioning. However, the question as to what this integration actually looks like or means in both theory and practice remains largely unexplored.[66]

2. Daly argues that his GEM model may have much to contribute not so much conceptually or substantively by telling people "what" to believe or "what" to think.[67] Rather it regards the highly unusual, unique, and even profound nature of the GEM model's contribution to the discussion and debate on human health and wellness. Noting that what constitutes clinical reasoning is a disputed subject as to the processes underlying accurate diagnosis, the importance of patient-specific versus population-based data, and the relation between virtue and expertise in clinical practice, Daly writes that his GEM model of clinical reasoning identifies and integrates the processes[68] of diagnosis, prognosis, and therapeutic decision-making. The model approaches inquiry with equal attention to the subject who investigates and the object under investigation. After identifying the structured operations of knowing and doing and relating these to a self-correcting cycle of learning, he correlates levels of inquiry regarding what-is-going-on and what-to-do to the practical and theoretical elements of clinical reasoning. He concludes that the model provides a methodical way to study questions regarding the operations of clinical reasoning as well as what constitute significant clinical data, clinical expertise, and virtuous health care practice.[69]

---

66. Daly "Model of Health," 431.

67. Structural change implies a dramatic shift in the way a government or entity operates. A key to effecting structural change is the dynamism that is inherent in that system. This usually requires major economic developments. Lonergan was aware of this as one can read in his CWL 15, 21. See also Chris Friel, "Evolution." As to structural changes in health care systems, Willich, "Advent," 1–6.

68. Daly's reference to the processes of diagnosis etc. can be related to the processes of Lonergan's cognitional theory and even extended to larger physical world processes explored by e. g. Michael Bretz in "Emergent." It is an implicit admission that processes inform his GEM model.

69. Daly "Model of Health," 431.

Fine, one may readily agree in principle with Daly's various suggestions, but I approach this "unique, profound" potential in terms of bringing about systematic change, as Lonergan himself suggests in his treatment of systematics in FS 7. With Tad Dunne, I address this through the prism of policy-making in FS 6, that is by transposing doctrines to healthcare policies when dealing with medical issues (Fig. 1). It is to be noted that judgment functions in all our knowing-doing operations but that its role is the central focus in both FS 3 and FS 7. Changes in nature and emergent probability are subject to constant processes.[70] FS 7 is concerned with how systems evolve and must be adapted to fit present, changing realities. Recall, for example, the work of Darwin, Mendel, Virchow and others' scientific discoveries and the processes that led them to their epoch-making contributions.

Relating the Insights of Ludwig von Bertalanffy and Other System Thinkers to Emergent Probability and to the Humanities

Daly has noted, as we saw, that there has not been much attempt to integrate the humanities into pre-intentional levels of biological functioning and the intentional levels of psycho-social functioning. Nor have there been relevant attempts to integrate the humanities into such models whereby they would interact and collaborate with the natural and human sciences in probing much deeper questions concerning the human good (see Appendix F). Daly's efforts in this endeavor are commendable. Others have attempted analogous types of *rapprochement* between system-thinking and global health.

In one of his papers, David H. Peters reviews the origins of systems thinking. Describing a range of the theories, methods, and tools, he notes that

> a common thread is the idea that the behavior of systems is governed by common principles that can be discovered and expressed. They each address problems of complexity, which is a frequent challenge in global health. The different methods and tools are suited to different types of inquiry and involve both qualitative and quantitative techniques.[71]

---

70. The sciences also "are in process." Lonergan notes that "it is difficult to see how the object of a science accounts for the unity of the science, since that object is not yet attained. Still though physics, chemistry, biology and so on are only probable, yet they develop as unities.... A science is a unity, and it embraces a totality, because the operations of the scientist, the acts corresponding to his objects, form a unified, interrelated group" subject to processes of development as illustrated in group theory. Lonergan, *Topics in Education*, 160.

71. Peters, "Application of Systems Thinking," abstract.

Appealing to von Bertalanffy's insights, as well as those of the anthropologist Gregory Bateson, Murray Gell-Mann and Kenneth Arrow (the latter two helped define complex adaptive systems), Peters goes on to say that "Much of the work in systems thinking has involved bringing together scientists from many disciplinary traditions, in many cases allowing them to transfer methods from one discipline to another . . ., or to work across and between disciplinary boundaries."[72] These efforts were possible due to creative types learning through a wide variety of stakeholders, including researchers and those affected by trans-disciplinary research. Peters concludes by emphasizing that explicit models used in systems thinking provide new opportunities to "continuously test and revise our understanding of the nature of things, including how to intervene to improve people's health."[73]

It is important to note some developments in Bertalanffy's general system theory (GST) to which both Lonergan and Daly appeal. First, GST and cybernetics were and are still often confused. Bertalanffy was concerned with first order cybernetics. Nonetheless, his "perspectivist" epistemology is said to be relevant with regard to developments in second-order cybernetics.[74]

Secondly, some scholars link Lonergan's views on emergent probability with the evolution of systems.[75] This parallels Daly's own efforts to relate common-sense experience in the medical field to statistical laws. Given large numbers of events and long periods of time, "it is probable that schemes of recurrence, though unlikely, will occur and set the stage for more elaborate schemes to follow. This theory serves as the basis for both the stability and the evolution of the universe, considered as intelligible and as supporting the development of intelligence."[76]

---

72. Peters, "Application of Systems Thinking," para. 5.

73. Peters, "Application of Systems Thinking," para. 17.

74. For an analysis of the complementarity of cybernetic and "organismic" trends in systems research within the unitary hermeneutical framework of "general systemology," see Skyttner, *General Systems*. On the history of Bertalanffy's "General Systemology," and its relationship to cybernetics, see Pouvreau and Drack, "History of Ludwig," 523–71.

75. Crysdale and Ormerod, *Creator God*, draw on the Thomist tradition as they examine Lonergan's emergent probability. Theirs is an evolutionary account of the universe in which purpose is to be found in finality—an upwardly directed dynamism characterized by increasing systematization. This involves the conditioned series of schemes of recurrence well-illustrated by, say, fusion cycles in stars to the Krebs cycle in the life of an organism.

76. Daly, "Theory of Health." 151. Note, however, that Lonergan reminds us in his "Lecture 2: Functional Specialty 'Systematic,'" that the FS approach "divides the process from data to results into different stages. Each stage pursues its own proper end in its own proper manner." He goes on to study the stages through which the Christian

Second-order Cybernetics

Second-order cybernetics, also known as the cybernetics of cybernetics, is the recursive application of cybernetics to itself. It was developed between 1968 and 1975 by Margaret Mead, Heinz von Foerster,[77] and others. It has been characterized as cybernetics where "circularity is taken seriously."[78] Needless to say, second-order cybernetics is analogous to Lonergan's treatment of the FS as a reduplicative feedback method whereby the mediated-healing phase is applied to reinvigorate and transform the mediating-creative phase. A conference was dedicated to this theme in July, 2019.[79] The conference, led by an interdisciplinary team of Seton Hall University scholars, asked and discussed the question of the extent to which Lonergan's work is relevant to cybernetics. It noted, for example, that one is struck by the resonances and interplay between the perspectives of Lonergan and second-order cybernetics, especially in terms of the scientist/observer interacting with and reflecting upon the subject, as well as the differences and contrasts between the two views. It sought to make the case that Lonergan can be understood in part as an early, illuminating figure for understanding second-order cybernetics itself.

Second-order cybernetics was developed and revised in the late 1960s and mid-1970s within almost the exact timeframe that Lonergan wrote *MiT*, in which he revisited some of the implications of values—a task he was forced to curtail due to his having been assigned to teach in Rome. The 1967 keynote address to the inaugural meeting of the American Society for

---

religion involved itself in systematic thinking—which has little to do with the Sermon on the Mount. He adds that "It is only on the basis of a full understanding and a complete acceptance of the developments in the contemporary notions of science, philosophy, and scholarship" that his account of the FS specialty systematics can be understood.

77. Heinz von Foerster, one of the originators of second-order cybernetics, attributes its rise to the attempts by cyberneticians to construct a model of the mind: "A brain is required to write a theory of a brain. From this follows that a theory of the brain, that has any aspirations for completeness, has to account for the writing of this theory. And even more fascinating, the writer of this theory has to account for her or himself. Translated into the domain of cybernetics, the cybernetician, by entering his own domain, has to account for his or her own activity. Cybernetics then becomes cybernetics of cybernetics, or second-order cybernetics." Foerster, *Understanding*, 289.

78. Glanville, "Second-order Cybernetics," 1380.

79. "Was Bernard Lonergan a Second-Order Cyberneticist?" was the theme of the Conference on Systemics, Cybernetics, and Informatics held in 2019 at Orlando, FL. Joseph Laracy argued that "cybernetics is inherently interdisciplinary; second-order cybernetics stresses reflective interaction of knowledge and action with the observer." Such themes are central to Lonergan's argumentations.

Cybernetics (ASC) by Margaret Mead, who had been a participant at the Macy Conferences, is a defining moment in the development of cybernetics. She characterized "cybernetics as a way of looking at things and as a language for expressing what one sees."[80]

I conclude FS 7 by noting that, as second-order cybernetics implies, scientists and physicians cannot afford to leave the personal dimensions of scientific research or healing to mere personal experience or to the collective wisdom of peers. Doing so can often lead to duplicating flawed approaches.

EIGHTH FUNCTIONAL SPECIALTY: SHARING UNIVERSAL VALUES AND HEALTH CARE ACROSS THE DIVIDES[81]

Achieving clarity in healthcare requires a transparent reporting of clinical data in health care, as Daly rightly points out. Transparency is defined as "lack of hidden agendas and conditions, accompanied by the availability of full information required for collaboration, cooperation, and collective decision making."[82] Transparency lets the light in. It is critical across the healthcare spectrum. There has been a loud and clear call for greater transparency in medicine, requiring a willingness to share information upon which clinical decisions are based. Transparency touches everything from how physicians practice medicine to how information is shared with patients and how hospitals gather and report outcomes. It should provide clarity to physicians and promote trust among patients and lead to long-term improvements in outcomes. To bridge the transparency divide, physicians need a thorough understanding of clinical evidence and the facts about the risks and harms associated with treatment alternatives. Achieving clarity in healthcare requires a transparent reporting of clinical data in health care, as Daly stresses.

---

80. See "Second-order Cybernetics," para. 6; Mead, "Cybernetics of Cybernetics," 2. One may add that "maintenance of health and the development of diseases are the result of complex dynamic interactions. Systems Medicine is the application of systems biology approaches to medical research and medical practice. Its objective is to integrate a variety of biological/medical data at all relevant levels of organization using the power of computational and mathematical modelling, from the level of inter-and-intracellular molecular networks of the cell to the levels of the interdependence of humans and their environments." "Systems Medicine," para. 4.

81. Albert Schweitzer rejected self-seeking to serve the poor in Africa. Lonergan's foundations apply to personal and communal ways whereby converted people such as Schweitzer or Mother Teresa's followers dedicate their lives to serve others.

82. Oettgen, "Transparency in Healthcare," 2.

At times, national or international clinical practice guidelines, supported by professional organizations, have issued conflicting recommendations for clinical care; this may be due to inconsistencies in the guideline development process. These inconsistencies can include the methods whereby relevant evidence is identified, appraised for quality and relevance, and interpreted. Differences may also occur in the translation of the evidence into practical recommendations for the target audience. There is a need for high-quality evidence-based clinical practice guidelines supporting recommendations. Developing a clinical practice guideline is a vast and time-consuming undertaking, often relying on experts in the field to volunteer their time as part of the guideline panel. The constitution of a guideline panel may influence the strength and focus of a recommendation whereby potential financial or intellectual conflicts may vitiate the process of impartially implementing the guidelines. Here human biases may also interfere.

Healing our Biases—Personally and Collectively—In and Out of Clinical Practice

Much of society today is dysfunctional. Developing nations and their inhabitants face many handicaps. Unless the GEM-FS world provides more than theoretical "answers" to such problems, it will fail in its task. The FS's cooperative potential should be implemented to remedy our dysfunctions. A long-term GEM-FS strategy has to be in place and periodically revised. Religious conversion implies self-giving. Intra-interfaith GEM-FS processes would translate faith into action so as to help people address concrete situations and help them balance their rights and duties. To combat the blind biases "out there," we must first monitor those within. We must reconcile the demands of a pure desire to know[83] with everyone's need for love. The great or ordinary saints and the immortal tale of *A Christmas Carol* can help us monitor our deeper self. As Scrooge is visited by the ghosts of the past, the present, and the future, and as Marley frees Scrooge from avarice—turning him from his misanthropy into a philanthropist, so GEM-FS can help us counter our illusions by dealing with overspecialization. While Dickens found hope in a miser's conversion, Lonergan "devised" a method that seriously tackles our biases. GEM-FS promotes the ideals of personal

---

83. The operator immanent in persons propels development and makes for the emergence of higher integrations. (*Insight*, 490–92, 494–504). The operator of the cognitive development is the pure desire to know (*Insight*, 555). Development is in accord with the metaphysical principle of "finality," which is the immanent intelligibility of emerging world process (*Insight*, 470–76).

conversion so as to address larger needs. GEM-FS adherents cannot ignore this—unless they would forfeit GEM-FS' larger implications. An untoward event had turned a Scrooge into an unsociable miser. As the ghosts help him understand why he had become so embittered, so GEM-FS can help people cut off from their deeper, inner selves become healers of others personally and collectively.

CONCLUSION

I have argued that Lonergan's GEM-FS method is a key discovery that, when correctly understood and executed, can help mankind find common solutions to such problems as healthcare. While Daly contends that his GEM model of health can help solve some fundamental issues in this area, I have sought to upgrade his one-phase GEM model within *MiT*'s diphase process approach, one that transforms horizons. This involves judgments of value relying in part on "normative theories of health."[84] In doing so, I have referred to the memory device AIRR for remembering Lonergan's fourfold transcendental precepts, be attentive, be intelligent, be rational, and be responsible, which encapsulate the basic structure of critical-realistic thinking (as noted in Fig. 1 and stressed in Parts II to IV). I have reprised AIRR in reduplicative-inverse fashion in addressing *MiT*'s second phase so as to engage in a mRNA-conversion analogue that involves the full implications of Lonergan's and Doran's accounts of psychic, intellectual, moral, and religious conversions.

---

84. Daly, *Theoretical Medicine*, 15–40, addresses the incommensurability between naturalist and normative approaches.

Appendix A[1]

Lonergan's Early Works as Prefiguring his Later Concerns in Insight and MiT

In his early essay. "St. Thomas' Thought on *Gratia Operans*,"[2] Lonergan sketched the content of *Summa Theologica*, la 2ae q. IIIa. 2c. He drew the implications of the declining importance of habitual grace in Saint Thomas's successive works. In *Gratia Operans*, meant to prepare for an inquiry into his concept of actual grace as operative and cooperative, Lonergan treats three main points:

1. The general nature of habit.
2. Habitual grace as a *gratia sanans*.
3. The infusion of habitual grace as a promotion.

Generally speaking, these three topics correspond to Aquinas's initial position in the *Sentences*, his development of it in the *De Veritate*, and a further development which begins with the *Contra Gentiles* and is consummated in the *Summa Theologica*. Lonergan concludes, first, that in the *Summa*, actual grace is operative as well as cooperative. Aquinas defines the gifts of the Holy Spirit in terms of connaturality and an external principle of motion. Lonergan adds:

> Second, there is development with regard to the necessity of virtues. In the *Sentences*, this necessity is merely in terms of

---

[1]. This and other appendices (and my entire text) are a series of clarifications as to my attempts to complement Daly's perceptive development of a GEM model with GEM-FS process.

[2]. An adaptation of his doctoral dissertation, *Grace and Freedom*, published in *Theological Studies* in 1942.

statistical law; in the *De Veritate*, statistical law gives way to relative impossibility. Coincident with this development is a fuller grasp of the nature of Pelagianism and the transfusion of 12th century Augustinian thought into the Thomist synthesis. Third, there is development with regard to the prevenient action of grace on free will. In the *Sentences* and the *De Veritate* the free acts that take place in justification are informed by the infused grace; in the *Contra Gentiles* the "provenience" of grace is expressed in terms of *motus moventis* and *motus mobile*. In the *Summa* this terminology is developed on the analogy of Aristotelian physics and the motion of free will as well as its information is attributed to the simultaneously infused habitual grace.[3]

Lonergan's articles on *Verbum: Word and Idea in Aquinas*[4] touched on the cognitional theories of Plato, Aristotle, Augustine and Aquinas. In *Verbum*, Lonergan goes so far as to say

> Just as Thomist thought is an ontology of knowledge inasmuch as intellectual light is referred to its origin in uncreated Light, so too it is more than an embryonic epistemology inasmuch as intellectual light reflectively grasps its own nature and the commensuration of that nature to the universe of reality. . . .. In the measure one grasps the character and implication of the act by which intellectual light reflects by intellectual light upon intellectual light to understand itself and pronounce its universal validity, in that measure, one grasps one of the two outstanding analogies to the procession of an infinite Word from an infinite Understanding.[5]

In turn, in *Insight*, Lonergan develops an epistemology and a metaphysics commensurate with grasping what is meant in Catholic theology by a natural knowledge of God. In his structure of the human good,[6] (see fig. 2) "operation" denotes the actuation of one's basic invariant mode of knowing-doing; "cooperation" refers to how persons or groups work together in institutions to achieve the good. *MiT* involves both a way upwards (a mediating-creative phase that grasps the problems of history) and a way downwards (a mediated-healing phase challenging individuals and groups not only to understand problems but to find solutions). I have argued throughout this text that *MiT*'s mediated-healing phase opens up vast vistas to help upgrade Daly's pioneering work. Understanding Lonergan's insightful critique of Aquinas is a helpful step in doing so.

3. Lonergan, *Grace and Freedom*, 65.
4. Published between 1946–49.
5. Lonergan, *Verbum*, 87.
6. Lonergan, *MiT*, 48. See fig. 2.

Appendix B

Why "GEM-FS Process" Accurately Designates Lonergan's Achievement and his Method's Potential: Exaggerating in Interpreting "the Gap" Left Open at the End of Insight

Following upon the brief overview of Lonergan's lifework in Appendix A, I will now comment on a statement I made in the text that when assigned to teach in Rome, Lonergan realized that *Insight*, for all its merits, could have left him open to a charge that *Insight* was, to use a colloquialism, merely a "whack-a-mole" effort. Of course, I am exaggerating here to make a point.

Colloquially, "whack-a-mole" denotes a repetitious, futile task: each time a problem is dealt with, yet another task/problem crops up. The author Catherine B. King has used the "whack-a-mole" colloquialism in a Lonergan discussion group to warn us against the danger of a person's philosophical "hyper-objectivist foundations" being implicitly at work—thus clouding his/her stated views.[1] Such views, King argues, are tacitly mixed in—bleeding-up from below, as it were. They tend to confuse, misguide, or derail the more topical issue under discussion. In keeping with King's views, I argue that to reverse counter-positions Lonergan offers us the GEM-FS alternative—one that includes a distinctly differentiated view that points to an awareness of omissions as well as to the unacknowledged biases functioning in one's thinking.

---

1. The "whack-a-mole" expression, as used by King, means addressing foundational issues as they arise without distinguishing them from topical concerns. This leads to many types of confusion, provoking heated discussions. King uses Lonergan's view on counter-positions to reject such hyper-objectivist "foundations." See Lonergan, *Insight*, 413–15.

King adds that counter-positions have to be addressed on two levels: foundational and topical. This means that if the tacit foundational issues are present and cannot be approached directly (for many reasons), then they keep bubbling up in various ways. This presents us with "a jumble of topical issues influenced here and there by a veritable soup of foundational issues." One is then left with the alternatives of a) leaving the discussion, b) trying "to distinguish tacit foundations from the topical issue itself so that it can be approached again later from having its philosophical undergrowth, or c) playing whack-a-mole."[2]

When foundational issues are not clearly and accurately addressed, separately and on their own ground, all sorts of blocks and confusions easily ensue, leading to heated arguments but to no solution. Lonergan teaches us to avoid sloppy thinking. It is therefore important to note that scientists, competent in their field, often operate from unacknowledged, uncritical philosophical foundations. What is, in fact, required to avoid this dilemma is a slow reading of the masters of philosophical discussions" so that one can come to know one's own interior processes so as to correct one's own philosophical errors that influence one's foundational comportment." King concludes that the two-level problem is probably behind Lonergan's oft-repeated statement that he could not write *Insight* into every essay of his. That is why he urges his readers to learn how to achieve "self-appropriation." Self-appropriation involves the processes of coming to terms with one's own underlying counter-positions, and countering the biases and distorted forms of development that tend to hinder GEM-FS's proper functioning. The processes Lonergan used to develop his particular set of scientific practices became for him "the first and basic task of philosophy."[3] These processes were also

> The transformation of a traditional model for conceiving the relationships among philosophic discourses. Lonergan's "first philosophy" is not first in a hierarchy of discourses, but first in an order of methodical controls; it is not ontologically but methodologically basic and prior to particular sciences, it is first as the science of sciences in a context where science are defined by their methodologies rather than by their subjects.[4]

The GEM-FS process approach sketched in *MiT*, chapters 1 and 5, outlines how the FS are based on the basic structure, function, and activities of human, intentional consciousness. Crucial to *MiT*'s approach is Lonergan's

2. King, in the Lonergan discussion group.
3. Wilkins, *Before Truth*, 132.
4. Wilkins, *Before Truth*, 132.

distinction between the mediating-creating and mediated-healing phases. Only in the latter phase can one address the changes needed in persons' and scholars' foundational reality brought about by the conversions. I have argued that Daly's GEM model overlooks some of these foundational-topical issues—partly due to his not sufficiently adverting to *MiT*'s transitioning from the mediating to the mediated phase.

Appendix C

How Daly Compares the Definition of Disease Given by Daniel Sulmasy, MD, with Lonergan's Theory of Cognitional Structure and Intentionality—a Helpful Step

This appendix points to some original contributions Daly makes for applying Lonergan's method in the treatment of disease. Daly has identified some of the ethical dilemmas facing medical practitioners, philosophers, and society in general. But I have argued that his is also part of a larger *ongoing process*[1] doctors face when assessing and treating bodily functions—that is, his "GEM model" implicitly points to or begs for a more dynamic "GEM-FS process." Part of what is needed in such a process is the ability to access one's interiority, one's deeper self, the spiritual dimensions of life so as to be able to communicate on a level that does not ignore differences in beliefs (as briefly explored in Appendix D). The present appendix first asks "To what extent are bodily and spiritual or interiority processes linked in actual life?"[2] Daly writes that

> Defining disease and delineating its boundaries is a contested area in contemporary philosophy of medicine. The leading naturalistic theory faces a new round of difficulties related to defining a normal environment alongside normal organismic functioning and to delineating a discrete boundary between

---

1. See *MiT*, 29, and *Insight*, 602, on ongoing processes proceeding from particular viewpoints.
2. Buddhism teaches processes of cause and effect (*karma*) based on an immanent world view. Its forms of meditation such as in Christian Zen help one reconcile the immanent and transcendent aspects of life.

risk factors and disease. Normative theories face ongoing and seemingly intractable difficulties related to value pluralism and the problematic relation between theory and practice.[3]

Daly argues for an integral—as opposed to a hybrid—philosophy of health based on Lonergan's notion of GEM "that provides a way to settle these difficulties dynamically and comprehensively, both in theory, by orienting functional and statistical investigation toward an explanatory ecological viewpoint, and in practice, by framing critiques in relation to the normativity intrinsic to all human inquiry.[4] Daly adds that for Lonergan, the structure of

> classical empirical method . . . operates as a pair of scissors. Its upper blade consists in a heuristic structure . . . [that is] a set of generalities demanding specific determination, and such determination comes from the lower blade of working hypotheses, precise measurements, empirical correlations, deductions of their implications, experiments to test the deduced conclusions, revisions of the hypothesis, and so *da capo*.[5]

Referring to Lonergan's argument[6] on the complementarity between classical and statistical investigations, Daly concludes that it should be "evident that the whole of science, with logic thrown in, is a development of intelligence that is complementary to the development named common sense."[7] Daly defines disease and illness in terms derived from Lonergan's theory of cognitional structure and intentionality. He compares his definition with Daniel Sulmasy's definition of disease based on a theory of natural kinds. For Sulmasy,

> A disease is a class of states of affairs of individual members of a living natural kind X, that:
>
> 1. disturbs the internal biological relations (law-like principles) that determine the characteristic development and typical history of members of the kind, X,
> 2. in a pattern of disturbance shared with at least one other member of the kind, X.

---

3. Daly, "Integral Approach to Health Science," 15.
4. Daly, "Integral Approach to Health Science," 23, referring to Lonergan, *Insight*, 600.
5. Lonergan, *Insight*, 600.
6. Lonergan, *Insight*, 126–43.
7. Daly, "Integral Approach to Health Science," 15, referring to Lonergan, *Insight*, 200–203.

3. The aim of this classification must be to provide at least a provisional basis for explaining the causes and/or natural history of a disturbance in the internal biological relations of the affected members of X (and, if X is a self-reflective natural kind, can serve as an explanation of the illness of those so affected),
4. and at least some individuals of whom (or which) this class of states of affairs can be predicated are, by virtue of that state, inhibited from flourishing.[8]

Daly develops Sulmasy's definitions of disease and injury in analogical ways. In doing so, he focuses on three pairs of terms in Sulmasy's and Lonergan's respective standpoints: (1) "class of states of affairs" and "conjugates"; (2) "members of natural kinds" and organisms; and (3) "internal biologic relations" and "schemes of recurrence."[9] Daly compares what Lonergan means by "state of health" to Sulmasy's "states of affairs of individual(s)," noting that "where class functions logically, conjugates function intelligibly or formally." For Sulmasy, a "pattern of disturbance" requires at least two instances to qualify as a disease. This requirement appears to be a matter of definition—implying that a class is a set with two or more members and not a matter of medical insight.

For Lonergan, conjugates are formulations based on insight into data as intelligible, either sensibly as related to us or formally as related to one another. What Sulmasy calls "a pattern of disturbance" is, for Lonergan, an example of data as intelligible. For Lonergan, the relation of understanding to experience is primarily a matter of insight into data as intelligible and secondarily a matter of abstracting concepts. Lonergan refers to the process of conjugate formation as "enriching abstraction," emphasizing the unity of cognitive operations, both on the side of the object and the side of the subject.

Besides relations (conjugates), another fundamental term of Lonergan's theory is "thing," which he defines as a concrete "unity-identity-whole" grasped by insight into data "in their individuality and in the totality of their aspects."[10] Lonergan differentiates things according to explanatory genera and species based on emergent probability as opposed to mechanist determinism.[11] Organisms are higher order things characterized by increasingly flexible schemes of recurrence emerging (evolving) according to verifiable laws of biologic, psychic, and rational development.[12] But organisms are also

---

8. Quoted in Daly, *Theoretical Medicine*, 38; see also 15–40.
9. Sulmasy, "Diseases and Natural Kinds," 492, 496.
10. Lonergan, *Insight*, 270.
11. Lonergan, *Insight*, 280–81.
12. Lonergan, *Insight*, 479–85.

concrete individual things, related intelligibly (rather than conceptually) to similar organisms by virtue of the act of insight into conjugate forms. Natural kinds would "occur" as conjugate forms in Lonergan's terms; individual members (organisms) "exist." Lonergan's analysis of the scholastic notions of substance and subsistence is pertinent in this regard. Quoting Cajetan, he asks, "What is the concept that you utter, humanity or man?" If it is just matter and form, then what you conceive in these data is humanity. If it is the matter and form of these very data as a determination of being, the concept that you utter is a man. While humanity is abstract, man is concrete. "Humanity is a principle limiting the being to being a man."[13]

Things develop and so does our understanding, of both things and relations. The organism is the same thing at each stage of its development; e.g., fetus, infant, child, adult. The disordered scheme of recurrence, or disease, called malaria, for instance, which literally means "bad air" was at first understood on the basis of that literal meaning. Medical researchers came to a more scientific understanding of malaria but the experiential conjugate of the disease has remained the same. Our understanding of disease and our formulations of explanatory conjugates develop in detail and precision. This is development in understanding; it does not make disease a thing.

Daly writes that Sulmasy's term, "internal biologic relations (law-like principles),[14] is similar to Lonergan's "schemes of recurrence," which considered abstractly are combination(s) of classical laws.[15] However, schemes of recurrence emerge and develop in a flexible (non-systematic) sequence as opposed to biologic principles. The latter are said to "determine" development and natural history. Additionally, Daly writes that schemes of recurrence are ordered generically in the following fashion: "rationality > psychology > biology > chemistry > physics."[16] This is Daly's way of interpreting Lonergan's view that higher order schemes, while dependent on lower order schemes, flexibly integrate them.[17]

Whereas Sulmasy separates definitions of disease and injury, Lonergan enables us to define disease in terms of schemes of recurrence showing the fundamental similarity between the two. Daly notes that "Even minor physical injury affects the whole organism, including biological relations and an organism's response to inflammation." Pursuing Lonergan's

---

13. Lonergan, *Understanding and Being*, 152–53.
14. Sulmasy, "Diseases and Natural Kinds," 505.
15. Lonergan, *Insight*, 141.
16. Daly, "Theory of Health," 150.
17. Lonergan, *Insight*, 280–83.

schemes-of-recurrence approach, Daly says that the conditions of disruption in an organism, "may stand in as diagnoses for disordered schemes with which they are statistically associated."[18] They are often the focus of therapeutic attention; e. g, hypertension, tobacco use, hypercholesterolemia.

While "states of affairs," in analytic terms, are descriptive of what is or may be the case, "states" for Lonergan are explanatory in terms of "probabilities associated with classes of events," among which are schemes of recurrence. For example, "John has a fever" describes a state of affairs; i.e., "John has a fever but he should recover, based on these factors." This involves a judgment regarding John's "state of health," which carries explanatory (prognostic) as well as descriptive import.[19] Daly concludes this topic by saying that "cure is therapy of the patient as object. Care is therapy of the patient as subject. By patient, I mean someone who suffers an illness or injury." He adds that he has "provided a heuristic definition of health, related to the notion of the good and defined disease in terms of disordered schemes of recurrence" etc.

---

18. Daly, "Theory of Health," 147, early version.
19. Lonergan, *Insight*, 81, 105.

Appendix D

Some Suggestions for Reconciling Eastern-Western Views on Theology and Medicine Based on an Assessment of the Polymorphism of Consciousness in Life and Scholarship

The polymorphism of consciousness and the resulting imprecisions of words and expressions ever remain a challenge for communication. It affects transcultural, interreligious discussions. Accessing one's interiority (as an apophatic) in ways the later Lonergan outlined for us, in his section "Foundational Reality" of *MiT*, for example, may prove a stabilizing anchor for reconciling East-West differences.

Appendix C noted that for Lonergan, the structure of classical empirical method consists in a heuristic structure—a set of generalities that operates in heuristic fashion as pair of scissors. In his chapter on "Metaphysics as Dialectic," Lonergan extends his notion of the scissors movement to the interpretation of texts. He notes that in this case the upper blade

> Has two components, which respectively regard meaning and expression. Both components are concretely universal, for they regard the potential totality of meanings, and the potential totality of modes of expression. . . . The relativism with which hermeneutics has been affected arises not because scholars have been neglecting the lower blade . . . that consists in the extraordinary array of techniques for dealing with the documents and monuments of the past, but because there has not been available an appropriate upper blade.[1]

---

1. Lonergan, *Insight*, 600.

Applying "the Upper Blade" to Interfaith Endeavors and Spiritualities

GEM-FS clarifies how the upper blade can help us interpret so as to interrelate Eastern and Western views of philosophies and religion. GEM-FS is close to Eastern philosophies in not excluding religion when analyzing consciousness; its judgments are open to mystic insights.[2] One uses embodied intentionality in constituting one's world; the eye of love responding to God's love helps one live ethically. GEM-FS saves us from intuitionism by having us affirm our actions as our own. Knowledge is discursive, not intuitive.[3] The intelligible is what we expect to grasp when we ask how new things emerge out of the old. Aggregates of acts of knowing are taken up into successively higher syntheses. Emergence is the process in which otherwise coincidental manifolds of lower conjugate acts "invite the higher integration effected by higher conjugate forms"[4] Lonergan does not downplay the distinction between self and the other; intersubjectivity serves as a matrix for one's self-realization. Lonergan challenges us to construct the human good in ways that go beyond cognition to the plane of ethical and/or transcultural action. Let us briefly address such complexities from the viewpoint of the polymorphism of consciousness which has given rise to many interpretations and theologies as to how one lives an authentic religious life in various contexts, in various traditions.

In his *Christianity with an Asian Face: Asian American Theology in the Making*, Peter C. Phan draws on the twin themes of liberation and inculturation. He explicates a new theology forged in the cauldron of the encounter between two vastly different cultures. Phan explores his own Vietnamese roots to sketch the contours of an Asian-American theology, an expression of faith caught between the Dragon and the Eagle. One may compare Phan's efforts in theology to trying to learn from the wisdom of ancient Chinese medicine which diagnoses illness by asking about the history of the illness and about such things as the patient's taste, smell, and dreams. Conclusions are drawn from the quality of the voice; note is made of the color of the face and of the tongue. The most important part of the investigation, however, is the examination of the pulse. Wang Shuhe, who wrote the "Pulse Classic," lived in the third century BCE; innumerable commentaries were written

---

2. Lonergan, *MiT*, 29, refers to a mystic differentiation of consciousness as being that of mystic who "withdraws into the *ultima solitudo*, [dropping] the constructs of culture" as well as "the whole complicated mass of mediating operation to return to a new, mediated immediacy of his subjectivity reaching for God."

3. Lonergan, *MiT*, 238.

4. Lonergan, *Insight*, 477.

on his work. The pulse is examined in several places, at different times, and with varying degrees of pressure. The operation may take as long as three hours. It is often the only examination made, and it is used both for diagnosis and for prognosis. Not only are the diseased organs ascertained, but the time of death or recovery may be foretold.[5]

The Chinese materia medica has always been extensive and consists of vegetable, animal (including human), and mineral remedies. There were famous herbals from ancient times, but all these, to the number of about a thousand, were embodied by Li Shijen in the compilation of *Bencao gangmu* (the "Great Pharmacopoeia") in the sixteenth century CE. This work, in fifty-two volumes, has been frequently revised and reprinted and is still authoritative. The use of drugs is mainly to restore the harmony of the *yin* and the *yang* and is also related to such matters as the five organs, the five planets, and the five colors. The art of prescribing is therefore complex. Among the drugs taken over by Western medicine from the Chinese are rhubarb, iron (for anemia), castor oil, kaolin, camphor, and *Cannabis sativa* (Indian hemp).

I have argued that GEM-FS offers us global perspectives to help heal the world. In some of my previous publications, I have appealed to interfaith dialogues, based on loving faith rather than divisive beliefs.[6] A loving faith can help us understand how the levels of ethics might become operative so as to establish a moral ground for interdisciplinary, interfaith studies mindful of evolutionary dimensions. GEM-FS's inclusive approach can help us link several key notions informing this text such as universal values. Let us note, for instance, that in the *Chandogya Upanishad*, 3, 14, one reads:

> This Atman (human being) that I have in my heart is smaller than a grain of rice, smaller than an oat, smaller than a seed . . .
> This Atman that I have in my heart is greater than the globe . . . greater than all spaces of the Universes. In it are . . . all contained; it embraces all . . .
> He who has attained to this knowledge, for him verily there is no more doubt.
> This Atman that I have in my heart, it is this Brahman.

---

5. See "Traditional Medicine and Surgery in Asia: China."

6. Lonergan appeals to W. Cantwell Smith's distinction between an inclusive faith and divisive beliefs. *MiT*, 115–17.

Relating Global Spiritualities to Kierkegaard and to the Practice of Science

Without getting into complex interpretations of Hinduism and Buddhism, we can ascertain that like the three transcendence-oriented Religions of the Book, the immanently-oriented Eastern religions can help get people of diverse cultural, religious and experiential backgrounds agree on the importance of the heart in reconciling humans. Only through genuine reconciliations can humans begin to live a GEM-FS process open to faith. Buddhists speak of mindful living, of mindfulness. Such a mindfulness developed in East Asia, can serve as a modern bridge for contemporary interfaith encounters. "Mindfulness is the energy of being aware and awake to the present moment. It is the continuous practice of touching life deeply in every moment of daily life. To be mindful is to be truly alive, present and at one with those around you and with what you are doing."[7] We bring our body and mind into harmony. Such harmony is a necessary background for authentically evaluating the damage we humans have caused on the planet. This book would extend such mindfulness to interfaith, transcultural efforts to pursue the art of living faithful lives and/or of living, for example, according to the principles of *Feng-Shui* (literally "wind and water").

Feng-Shui is the ancient Chinese art of facilitating the flow of *ch'i* (life's animating force permeating one's physical surroundings, home, the rivers roads, trees, and all people). *Feng-Shui* helps people work with things as they are so as to enhance one's life by bringing it into harmony with its surroundings. It is a traditional Chinese concept linking human destiny to the environment. It is part and parcel of many aspects of Chinese and Japanese life but also offers us a helpful intercultural bridge for restoring harmony between nature and humans. I cannot here go into all the implications of mindful living or of *Feng-Shui*. I do note that these implications are important to our inclusive "GEM-FS-bridging-method" which seeks to integrate religious and cultural symbols with evolutionary insights into ethics. An inclusive notion of faith, in contrast to divisive beliefs, is crucial to fostering healing dialogue across the planet. One cannot but agree with Steven Greer's observation that "Alas, our technology has marched ahead of our spiritual and social evolution, making us, frankly, a dangerous people."[8] In the light of Greer's sobering remarks, Daly is to be commended for his attention to higher integrations which he relates to weather patterns, to evolution and the roles of schemes of recurrence. He writes that a

---

7. Thich Nhat Hanh, "Be Mindful," 2.
8. Greer, Internet quote 179318.

Weather pattern on the face of the earth varies on any given calendar day from year to year, but generally conforms to a seasonal pattern over a period of months, which relates in turn to the systematically ordered orientation of the earth in cycling the sun every year, other things being equal. . . . Unlike these relatively stable cycles, the cycle of learning, augmented by empirical method over the past 500 years, more readily discloses the dynamic potentiality in the unfolding of world order for the development of new types of things and schemes.[9]

The Need for Higher Integrations

While, as Daly notes, we need higher integrations in the complex tasks facing humanity, I have situated my version of "higher integrations" within a more encompassing view of Lonergan's interlocking series of interdependent sets and within interreligious categories not oblivious of the apophatic side of spirituality.[10] Wilfred Bion (1897–1979), a British psychiatrist, excelled in this area. Bion's observations about the role of dynamic group processes are set out in books and papers written in the 1940s but compiled and published in 1961. He refers to recurrent emotional states of groups as "basic assumptions." He argues that "in every group, two groups are actually present: the work group, and the basic assumption group. The work group is concerned with aspects of group functioning and with the primary task of the group. It keeps the group anchored to a sophisticated and rational level of behavior."[11]

Bion drew deeply on the apophatic thought of Saint John of the Cross and Meister Eckart and applied it to contemporary epistemology and psychoanalysis. In a way reminiscent of Bion, in their paper, "Selfless self-transcendence in the clinical setting as a source of self-enhancement,"[12] Bnaya Amid, Lewis Aron and Eyten Bachar examine the paradox of selfless-self

---

9. Daly, "GEM Model of Health," 439.

10. For Lonergan, the conversions almost always come in incrementally. Moral conversion does not mean moral perfection, but the withdrawal from being closed upon oneself—a shift from a criterion of personal satisfaction to one based on values that transcend self- and group interests. Religious conversion is a process of withdrawal from ignoring the transcendent realm in which God is known and loved. It may or may not lead to mystical prayer. In the former case, it shares in the intensity of religious love and an adversity to evil.

11. Bion, *Experiences in Groups*, 66.

12. Bion, *Experiences in Groups*, 86. I have explored Bion's contributions in my *Empowering Philosophy and Science*.

transcendence, that is, how the self is enriched through self-renunciation. The authors discuss what enables being carried away without forethought into selfless-self-transcendence and how, eventually, these inadvertent surrenders create therapeutic shifts. They suggest that selfless moves towards patients is part of a latent mutual process with them—enabling the restoration of the self to an enriched form. This implies that, like the patients, analysts also encounter themselves in a truer way allowing them to become who they really are through selflessly transcending themselves.[13]

Lonergan's article "The Subject" begins with the statement that "Each of us lives in a world of his own,"[14] being confined within one's own horizon. He later notes that "The paradox of the existential subject extends to the good existential subject." It is by one's actions that one becomes good or evil. Lonergan insists that the determination of the good or evil of an action is in each case "the work of the free and responsible subject producing the first and only edition"[15] This may be related to "the paradox" found in Kierkegaard's understanding about an individual transcending one's self. For Kierkegaard, the supreme paradox of all thought is the attempt to discover something that thought cannot think. "This passion is at bottom present in all thinking, even in the thinking of an individual, in so far as in thinking he participates in something transcending himself. But habit dulls our sensibilities, and prevents us from perceiving"[16] the truth of our subjectivity open to the transcendent.

---

13. Amid et al., "Selfless Self-Transcendence," 16–36.
14. Lonergan, "Subject," 69.
15. Lonergan, "Subject," 69.
16. Kierkegaard, *Climacus*, 46.

Appendix E

Relating Health to the Thought of Gadamer

Dr. Daly and Robert Luby, MD, have both related their notions of health to the thought of Hans-Georg Gadamer. Daly skillfully ties his own notion of health to Lonergan's definition of the notion of being when he considers health, disease, illness, cure, care, and patient as a basic nest of terms. Referring to Lonergan's habit of naming an unknown, the "x" in order to guide an inquiry and to Lonergan's heuristic definition of the notion of being,[1] in the sense that being is the object intended in every question (those with answers, those without, those that are yet to be asked), Daly defines health in a similar fashion, heuristically as a notion rather than formally as a concept. It is what I intend to restore in getting "better." As such, health is intimately related to the notion of the good. In terms of common sense, health is a norm for living well, often taken for granted until something goes wrong.[2]

For Gadamer, "our conscious self-awareness remains largely in the background so that our enjoyment of good health is constantly concealed from us."[3] One may note here that in his "A Lonerganian Revision of the Goals of Medicine,"[4] Luby speculates on how Lonergan might revise the goals of medicine. Referring to Gadamer's statement that the goal of medicine "must be understood as an attempt to restore an equilibrium that has been disturbed,"[5] Luby, using Lonergan's terminology, proposes a set of more refined goals:

1. Daly, "Possiblity of Hope," 59.
2. Daly, "Theory of Health," 147, early version.
3. Gadamer, *Enigma of Health*, 112.
4. Luby, "Restorative Medicine," 150.
5. Gadamer, *Enigma of Health*, 36.

1. To increase the survival probability of physiological schemes of recurrence.
2. To reverse or reduce the effects of events that disrupt physiological schemes, and/or to increase the efficacy of defensive schemes of recurrence in order to increase the re-emergent probability of the original physiological schemes of recurrence.
3. To restore the function of the most foundational scheme of recurrence in a conditioned series of schemes of recurrence.[6]

In this context, recall that Lonergan wrote that Wilhelm Dilthey recognized the historical school's success; the "school" was nevertheless "far closer to idealist than to empiricist ideas and norms."[7] While Dilthey transposed Hegelian thought "from idealist *Geist* to human *Leben*" and thereby clarified how historians understand life's expressions, Lonergan dialectically transposed Gadamer's notion of the universal viewpoint. He did so in ways that can help us interpret the apophatic spiritualities of Hinduism, Buddhism, Christianity or the Sufis.

One may note here that medical science is continually evolving. New medications and treatments are being developed at a rapid pace. Like all biological systems, both disease-causing organisms and their victims evolve.[8] But because biological evolution is much slower than cultural change, many diseases arise from the mismatch of our bodies to modern environments.

---

6. Luby, "Restorative Medicine," 152.
7. Lonergan, *MiT*, 210.
8. Recent advances in molecular biology, neurobiology, and imaging have demonstrated important insights about the nature of neurological diseases. Systems biology employs tools developed in physics and mathematics such as nonlinear dynamics, control theory, and modeling of dynamics systems.

Appendix F

Fig. 2 Lonergan's Diagram on the Structure of the Human Good[1]

Individual		Social	Ends
Potentiality	Actuation		
Capacity, need	Operation	Cooperation	Particular good
Plasticity, perfectibility	Development, skill	Institution, role, task	Good of order
Liberty	Orientation, conversion	Personal relations	Terminal good

"Operation" denotes the actuation of one's basic invariant mode of knowing-doing; "cooperation" refers to how persons or groups work together in institutions to achieve the good. Notice that the three ends are aligned with the actuation of our potentialities. One should stress the mutual interdependence of the various elements cited in the Structure of the Human Good. This, as does Fig. 1, suggests the reduplicative feedback process at the heart of Lonergan's GEM-FS process approach.

1. Lonergan, *MiT*, 48.

Bibliography

Amid, Bnaya, et al. "Selfless Self-Transcendence in the Clinical Setting as a Source of Self-Enhancement." *The American Journal of Psychoanalysis* 80 (2020) 16–36.
Arendt, Hannah. *The Life of the Mind*. Boston: Mariner, 1981.
Barber, Gregory. "What's Confusing about Calling Covid-19 Cases 'Asymptomatic.'" *Wired*, June 11, 2020.
Bartlett, Jonathan. "Was the COVID-19 Virus Designed? The Computer *Doesn't* Know." https://www.discovery.org/a/was-the-covid-19-virus-designed-the-computer-doesnt-know/.
Bateson, Gregory. *Steps to an Ecology of Mind*. Chicago: University of Chicago, 2000.
Baum, Gregory. *Man Becoming*. New York: Herder & Herder, 1970.
"Be Mindful in Daily Life." https.thichnhathanhfoundation.org/be-mindful-in-daily-life.
Beckmann, Jacques, et al. "Copy Number Variants and Genetic Traits: Closer to the Resolution of Phenotypic to Genotypic Variability." *Nature Reviews Genetics* 8.8 (2007) 639–46.
Bernstein, Richard J. *Praxis and Action*. Philadelphia: University of Pennsylvania, 1971.
Bigirimana, Stanislas. *Patterns of Human Knowing in the Information Society: A Philosophical Study of the Epistemological Implications of the Information Revolution*. PhD diss., Heidelberg University, 2011.
Bion, Wilfred R. *Experiences in Groups and Other Papers*. London: Tavistock, 1961.
Braio, Frank, *Lonergan's Retrieval of the Notion of Human Being*. Lanham, MD: University Press of America, 1988.
Bretz, Michael. "Emergent Probability: A Directed Scale-Free Network Approach to Lonergan's Generic Model of Model of Development." https://arxiv.org/pdf/cond-mat/0207241.pdf.
Buber, Martin. *I and Thou*. 1923. Translated by Walter Kaufman. 2nd ed. New York: Scribner's, 1958.
Byrne, Patrick. "Lonergan, Evolutionary Science, and Intelligent Design." *Revista Portuguesa de Filosofia* 63.4 (2007) 893–918.
Chaitanya, K. V. "Structure and Organization of Virus Genomes." In *Genome and Genomics*. 1–30. Singapore: Springer, 2019.

Crowe, Frederick E. "An Expansion of Lonergan's Notion of Value." *Lonergan Workshop* 7 (1988) 35–58.

Crysdale, Cynthia, and Neil Ormerod. *Creator God, Evolving World*. Minneapolis: Fortress, 2013.

Daly, Patrick. "Common Sense and the Common Morality." *Theoretical Medicine and Bioethics* 35 (2014) 187–203.

———. "A Concise Guide to Clinical Reasoning." *International Journal of Public Health Policy and Health Services Research* 24 (2018) 1–22.

———. "The GEM Model: A Model of Health Based on Generalized Empirical Method." *European Journal of Patient Centered Healthcare* 7.3 (2019) 421–42.

———. "An Integral Approach to Health Science and Healthcare." *Theoretical Medicine and Bioethics* 38.1 (2017) 15–40.

———. "Palliative Sedation, Withholding Life-saving Treatment, and Aid in Dying: What Is the Difference?" *Theoretical Medicine and Bioethics* 36 (2015) 1–12.

———. "The Possibility of Hope." *Lonergan Worskhop* 25.2 (2013) 53–84.

———. "A Theory of Health Science and the Healing Arts Based on the Philosophy of Bernard Lonergan." *Theoretical Medicine and Bioethics* 30.2 (2009) 147–60.

———. "Transcendental Method in Action." *Method: Journal of Lonergan Studies* 7.2 (2016) 1–24.

Damasio, Antonio R. *Descartes' Error: Emotion, Reason and the Human Brain*. New York: Avon, 1994.

Darwin, Charles. *The Origin of Species by Means of Natural Selection*. 1st ed. 1859, Reprint, London: Murray, 1900.

Descartes, René. "Discourse on the Method." In *The Philosophical Writings of Descartes*, translated by John Cottingham et al., 1:111–51. Cambridge: Cambridge University Press, 1985.

"Dipti Gupta." https://writing.dawsoncollege.qc.ca/portfolio/dipti-gupta.

Dobzhansky, Theodosius. "Nothing in Biology Makes Sense except in the Light of Evolution." *The American Biology Teacher* 35 (1973) 125–29.

Doran, Robert. "Complicate the Structure: Notes on a Forgotten Precept." Paper presented at the 31st annual Boston College Workshop, 2004.

———. "Essays in Systematic Theology, 36: Functional Specialties for a World Theology." https://loneganresource.com/pdf/books/1/36%20-%20Functional%20Specialties%20for%20a%20World%20Theology.pdf.

———. *Subject and Psyche*. Lanham, MD: University Press of America, 1977.

———. "Subject, Psyche, and Theology's Foundations." *The Journal of Religion* 57 (1977) 267–87.

———. *Theology and the Dialectics of History*. Toronto: University of Toronto, 1990.

Dukes, Hunter. "Assembling the Mechanosphere: Monod, Althusser, Deleuze and Guattari." *Deleuze Studies* 10.4 (2016) 514–30.

Dunne, Tad. "Bernard Lonergan." *Internet Encyclopedia of Philosophy*. https://iep.utm.edu/lonergan/.

———. "Being in Love." *Method: Journal of Lonergan Studies* 13.2 (1995) 161–75.

Eldredge, Niles, and Marjorie Grene. *Interactions—The Biological Context of Social Systems*. New York: Columbia University, 1992.

Evans, David W., et al. "The Form of Causation in Health, Disease and Intervention: Biopsychosocial Dispositionalism, Conserved Quantity Transfers and Dualist Mechanistic Chains." *Medicine, Health Care, and Philosophy* 20.3 (2017) n.p.

https://www.researchgate.net/publication/312929055_The_form_of_causation_in_health_disease_and_intervention_biopsychosocial_dispositionalism_conserved_quantity_transfers_and_dualist_mechanistic_chains.

"Exon." https://en.wikipedia.org/wiki/Exon.

Fenton, Aron. "Allostery: An Illustrated Definition for the 'Second Secret of Life.'" *Trends Bichem Sci* 33.9 (2008) 420–25.

Fischer, Kathleen. "Religious Experience in Lonergan and Whitehead." *Religious Studies* 16 (October 2008) 69–79.

Flanagan, Joseph. *Quest for Self-Knowledge: An Essay in Lonergan's Philosophy*. Toronto: University of Toronto Press, 1997.

Foerster, Heinz von. *Understanding: Essays on Cybernetics and Cognition*. New York: Springer-Verlag, 2003.

Foucault, Michel. *The Foucault Reader*. Edited by Paul Rabinow. New York: Pantheon, 1984.

———. *Order of Things*. London: Tavistock, 1970.

Francis, Pope. "Address of His Holiness Pope Francis to the International Federation of Catholic Medical Associations (FIAMC) Gathered in Rome to Celebrate Their Consecration to the Sacred Heart of Jesus." http://www.vatican.va/content/francesco/en/speeches/2019/june/documents/papa-francesco_20190622_fiamc.html.

Frattaroli, Elio. *Healing the Soul in the Age of the Brain: Why Medication Is Not Enough*. New York: Penguin, 2001.

Frezza, Stephen, and David A. Nordquest. "Engineering Insight: The Philosophy of Bernard Lonergan Applied to Engineering. Philosophical and Educational Perspectives on Engineering and Technological Literacy." In *Philosophical and Educational Perspectives on Engineering and Technological Literacy*, edited by John Heywood, 2:17–28. Wicklow, Ireland: Reads, Main St. Bray, 2015. https://core.ac.uk/download/pdf/38939285.pdf.

Gadamer, Hans-Georg. *The Enigma of Health*. Stanford: Stanford University Press, 1996.

Ghaemi, Nassir. *The Rise and Fall of the Biopsychosocial Model*. Baltimore: John Hopkins University Press, 2010.

Glanville, Ranulph. "The Purpose of Second-order Cybernetics." *Kybernetes* 33.9/10 (2004) 1379–86. https://pdfs.semanticscholar.org/8a92/600c54967f99b020522cbdfbf6cfc364c401.pdf.

Green, Sara, and Henrik Vogt. "Personalizing Medicine: Disease Prevention." *Humana. Mente Journal of Philosophical Studies* 30.9 (2016) 1–42.

Grover, Fred, Jr. *Spiritual Genomics: A Physician's Deep Dive beyond Modern Medicine: Discovering Unique Keys to Optimizing DNA Health, Longevity, and Happiness*. Denver: Spiritual Genomics, 2019.

Halse, Scott Andrew. *Bernard Lonergan's Methodology and the Philosophy of Religion: Functional Specialization and Religious Diversity*. Lewiston, NY: Mellen, 2010.

Harrison, Reema, et al. "Addressing Unwarranted Clinical Variation: A Rapid Review of Current Evidence." *Journal of Evaluation in Clinical Practice* 25.1 (2019) 53–65.

Hobes, Aubrey. *Martin Buber: An Intimate Portrait*. New York: Viking, 1971.

Hood, Leroy, and Mauritio Flores. "A Personal View on Systems Medicine and the Emergence of Proactive P4 Medicine: Predictive, Preventive, Personalized and Participatory." *New Biotechnology* 29 (2012) 613–24.

Hosinski, Thomas E. "Lonergan and a Process Understanding of God." http://www.anthonyflood.com/hosinskilonerganprocessgod.htm.

Husserl, Edmund. *Logical Investigations*. 2 vols. Translated by John Niemeyer Findlay. London: Routledge, 2001.

"Intron." https://en.wikipedia.org/wiki/Intron.

James, William. *The Principles of Psychology*. New York: Holt, 1890.

"Johann Gregor Mendel (1822–1884): Father of Genetics." http://www.dnaftb.org/1/bio.html#:~:text=Gregor%20Mendel%2C%20through%20his%20work,as%20dominant%20or%20recessive%20traits.

Kanaris, Jim. "Calculating Subjects: Lonergan, Derrida, and Foucault." *Method: Journal of Lonergan Studies* 15.2 (1997) 135–50.

———. *Deference to the Other: Lonergan and Contemporary Continental Thought*. New York: State University of New York Press, 2000.

Khushf, George. "Health as Intra-systemic Integrity: Rethinking the Foundations of Systems Biology and Nanomedicine." *Perspectives in Biology and Medicine* 51.3 (2008) 432–49.

Kierkegaard, Soren. *Johannes Climacus, Philosophical Fragments*. Translated by H. V. and Edna Hong. Princeton: Princeton University Press, 1985.

King, Catherine. *Finding the Mind: Pedagogy for Verifying Cognitional Theory*. Lanham: MD: University Press of America, 2005.

Lakatos, Imre. *The Methodology of Scientific Research Programs*. Cambridge: Cambridge University Press, 1978.

Lamb, Matthew. *Solidarity With Victims: Toward a Theology of Social Transformation*. New York: Crossroad, 1982.

Laracy, Joseph, et al. "Was Bernard Lonergan a Second-Order Cyberneticist?" Paper presented at the 23rd World Multi-Conference on Systemics, Cybernetics, and Informatics, Orlando, Florida, July 6–9, 2019.

Liddy, Richard. *Transforming Light: Intellectual Conversion in the Early Lonergan*. Collegeville, MN: Liturgical, 1993.

Lonergan, Bernard. "The Analogy of Meaning." In *Philosophical and Theological Papers 1958–1964*, edited by Robert C. Croken et al., 83–212. *CWL* 6. Toronto: University of Toronto, 1996.

———. "Aquinas Today: Tradition and Innovation." In *A Third Collection*, edited by Frederick Crowe, 35–54. New York: Paulist, 1985.

———. "Belief: Today's Issue." In *A Second Collection*, edited by William Ryan and Bernard Tyrell, 87–100. Philadelphia: Westminster, 1974.

———. "Dialectic of Authority." In *A Third Collection*, edited by Frederick Crowe, 3–12. New York: Paulist, 1985.

———. "Dimensions of Meaning." In *Collection*, edited by Frederick Crowe, 252–67. Montreal: Palm, 1967.

———. *Early Works on Theological Method 1*. Edited by Robert Doran and Robert Crocken. *CWL* 22. University of Toronto, 2013.

———. "Existenz and Aggiornamento." In *Collection*, edited by Frederick Crowe, 240–51. Montreal: Palm, 1967.

———. *For a New Political Economy*. Edited by Philip McShane. *CWL* 21. Toronto: University of Toronto Press, 1998.

———. "The Future of Thomism." In *A Second Collection*, edited by William Ryan and Bernard Tyrell, 43–54. Philadelphia: Westminster, 1974.

———. *Grace and Freedom: Operative Grace in the Thought of St Thomas Aquinas*. CWL 1. Edited by Frederick Crowe and Robert Doran. Toronto: University of Toronto, 2000.

———. "Healing and Creating in History." In *A Third Collection*, edited by Frederick Crowe, 100–109. New York: Paulist, 1985.

———. "Horizons and Transpositions." In *Philosophical and Theological Papers, 1965-1980*, edited by Robert C. Croken et al., 409–32. CWL 17. Toronto: University of Toronto, 2004.

———. *The Incarnate Word*. Edited by Robert Doran and Jeremy Wilkins. CWL 8. Toronto: University of Toronto Press, 2016.

———. *Insight, a Study in Human Understanding*. Edited by Frederick Crowe and Robert Doran. CWL 3. Toronto: University of Toronto, 1997.

———. "Insight Revisited." In *A Second Collection*, edited by William Ryan and Bernard Tyrell, 263–78. Philadelphia: Westminster, 1974.

———. "Lecture 2: The Functional Speciality 'Systematics.'" In *Philosophical and Theological Papers, 1965-1980*, edited by Robert Crocken and Robert Doran, 301–12. CWL 17. Toronto: University of Toronto, 2004.

———. *Macroeconomic Dynamics: An Essay in Circulation Analysis*. Edited by Frederick G. Lawrence et al. CWL 15. Toronto: University of Toronto Press, 1999.

———. *Method in Theology*. 1st ed. New York: Herder & Herder, 1972.

———. "Moral Theology and Human Sciences." In *Philosophical and Theological Papers, 1965-1980*, edited by Robert Crocken and Robert Doran, 179–97. CWL 17. Toronto: University of Toronto, 2004.

———. "Natural Right and Historical Mindedness." In *A Third Collection*, edited by Frederick Crowe, 169–83. New York: Paulist, 1985.

———. "Philosophy and the Religious Phenomenon." In *Philosophical and Theological Papers 1965-1980*, edited by Frederick Crowe and Robert Doran, 391–408. CWL 17. Toronto: University of Toronto, 2004.

———. *Philosophy of God and Theology*. Philadelphia: Westminster Press, 1974.

———. "Prolegomena to the Study of the Emerging Religious Consciousness of Our Time." In *A Third Collection*, edited by Frederick Crowe, 55–73. New York: Paulist, 1985.

———. "The Subject." In *A Second Collection*, edited by William Ryan and Bernard Tyrell, 69–86. Philadelphia: Westminster, 1974.

———. "Theories of Inquiry." In *A Second Collection*, edited by William Ryan and Bernard Tyrell, 33–42. Philadelphia: Westminster, 1974.

———. *Topics in Education*. Edited by Robert Doran and Fred Crowe. CWL 10. Toronto: University of Toronto Press, 1993.

———. *Understanding and Being: The Halifax Lectures on Insight*. Edited by Mark and Elizabeth Morelli and Frederick Crowe. CWL 5. Toronto: University of Toronto, 1990.

———. *Verbum: Word and Idea in Aquinas*. Notre Dame: University of Notre Dame, 1967.

———. "The World Mediated by Meaning." In *Philosophical and Theological Papers 1965-1980*, edited by Frederick Crowe and Robert Doran, 107–18. CWL 17. University of Toronto, 2004.

Lovejoy, A. O. *The Great Chain of Being*. Cambridge: Harvard University Press, 1936.

Luby, Robert. "Restorative Medicine: Defensive Schemes and Re-emergent Possibilities." *Method, Journal of Lonergan Studies* 25.2 (2013) 139–68.
Marsh, James. *Lonergan in the World*. Toronto: University of Toronto, 2014.
———. "What's Critical about Critical Theory?" *Perspectives on Habermas*, edited by Lewis Edwin Hahn, 555–68. Chicago: Open Court, 2000.
Martinez, Julio. "Revisiting the Common Good in the Digital Age." *La Civilta Catolicca*, June 2, 2020.
Matthews, William A. *Lonergan's Quest: A Study of Desire in the Authoring of Insight*. Toronto: University of Toronto, 2005.
McCarthy, Michael H. *The Crisis of Philosophy*. New York: State University of New York Press, 1990.
———. "Towards a New Critical Center." *Method, Journal of Lonergan Studies* 15.2 (2017) 111–34.
McDonald, Mary Josephine. "Body-Psyche-Mind in the Self-Appropriation of the Subject: Complexifying Lonergan's Account of Nature and Supernature." PhD diss., University of Toronto, 2014.
McPartland, Thomas. Remarks on "Philosophy and the Religious Phenomenon." *Method, Journal of Lonergan Studies* 12.2 (1994) iv–vi.
———. "Philosophy of History and a Second Axial Age." *Sage Journal* 116.1 (2013) 19–49.
McShane, Phil. *The Future: Core Precepts in Supramolecular Method and Nanochemistry*. Vancouver: Axial, 2019.
———. *Futurology Express*. Vancouver: Axial, 2013.
———. "The Heart of Lonergan's Ethics." *Journal of Macrodynamic Analysis* 7 (2012) 59–93.
———. "The Positive Anthropocene Age: Seeding a New Popular Culture." Conference at the University of British Columbia, Vancouver, Canada, July 8–12, 2019. http://www.philipmcshane.org/forum/forums/reply/1949/.
McWhinney, Ian R. *Textbook of Family Medicine*. 3rd ed. Revised by Thomas Freeman. Oxford: Oxford University Press, 2009.
Mead, Margaret. "The Cybernetics of Cybernetics." In *Purposive Systems*, edited by Heinz von Foerster et al., 1–11. New York: Spartan, 1968.
Monod, Jacques. *Chance and Necessity*. New York: Vintage, 1972.
Morelli, Elizabeth A. "Post-Hegelian Elements in Lonergan's Philosophy of Religion." *Method: Journal Lonergan Studies* 12 (1994) 216–21.
Morelli, Elizabeth A., and Mark Morelli. *The Lonergan Reader*. Toronto: University of Toronto Press, 1997.
Morelli, Mark. "Lonergan's Unified Theory of Consciousness." *Method, Journal of Lonergan Studies* 17.2 (Fall 1999) 171–88.
Moss, Lenny. *What Genes Can't Do*. Cambridge: MIT Press, 2002.
Murray, Michael F. "Gregor Mendel and 21st Century Medicine." *Cardiology News*, February 23, 2012.
"Neuromorphic Computing." www.intel.com/content/www/us/en/research/neuromorphic-computing.html.
Oettgen, Peter. "Transparency in Healthcare: Achieving Clarity in Healthcare through Transparent Reporting of Clinical Data." DynaMed. https://www.ebsco.com/sites/g/files/nabnos191/files/acquiadam-assets/66751087.pdf.

Oyler, David. "The Philosophy of Consciousness: Method, Intelligence, Reality and Performance." www.davidoyler.org.

Panhuysen, Geert. "The Relationship Between Somatic and Psychic Processes Lessons from Freud's Project." *Annals of Academy of Sciences* 843.1 (1998) 20–42.

Pellauer, David, and Bernard Dauenhauer. "Paul Ricoeur." *The Standford Encyclopedia of Philosophy*. https://plato.stanford.edu/cgi-bin/encyclopedia/archinfo.cgi?entry=ricoeur.

Pellegrino, Edmund D., and David C. Thomasma. *A Philosophical Basis of Medical Practice*. New York: Oxford University Press, 1981.

Peters, David H. "The Application of Systems Thinking in Health: Why Use Systems Thinking?" 12.51 (2014). https://health-policy-systems.biomedcentral.com/articles/10.1186/1478-4505-12-51.

"Primary Process." www.ecologycenter.us/double-bind/primary-process.html.

Prouveau, David, and Manfred Drack. "On the History of Ludwig von Bertalanffy's 'General Systemology,' and on Its Relationship to Cybernetics." *International Journal of General Systems* 36.3 (2015) 281–37.

Pulchalski, Christina. "The Role of Spirituality in Health Care." *Baylor University Medical Center Proceedings* 4.4 (2001) 352–57.

Rahner, Karl. "Neue Ansprüche de Pastoraltheologie an die Theologie als Ganze." *Gregorianum* 50.3 (1969) 617–38.

Raymaker, John. *Bernard Lonergan's Third Way of the Heart and Mind: Bridging some Buddhist-Christian-Muslim-Secularist Misunderstandings with a Global Secularity Ethics*. Lanham, MD: Hamilton, 2016.

———. *A Buddhist-Christian Logic of the Heart*. Lanham, MD: Rowman & Littlefield, 2002.

———. *Empowering Bernard Lonergan's Legacy: Toward Implementing an Ethos for Inquiry and a Global Ethics*. Lanham, MD: University Press of America, 2013.

———. *Empowering Philosophy and Science with the Art of Love. Lonergan and Deleuze in the Light of Buddhist-Christian Ethics*. Lanham, MD: University Press of America, 2006.

———. *Empowering the Lonely Crowd*. Lanham, MD: University Press of America, 2003.

———. "Theory-Praxis of Social Ethics: The Complementarity between Bernard Lonergan's and Gibson Winter's Theological Foundations." PhD diss., Marquette University, 1977.

Raymaker, John, and Gerald Grudzen. *Pope Francis, Conscience of the World: Building Needed Bridges in a Troubled World*. Lanham, MD: Hamilton, 2020.

Raymaker, John, and Gerald Grudzen, with Joe Holland. *Spiritual Paths to An Ethical & Ecological Global Civilization: Reading the Signs of the Times with Buddhists, Christians, & Muslim*. Washington, DC: Pacem in Terris Press, 2013.

Raymaker, John, with Godefroid Mombula. *Bringing Bernard Lonergan down to Earth and into our Hearts and Communities*. Eugene, OR: Wipf & Stock, 2018.

Raymaker, John, with Ijaz Durrani. *Empowering Climate-Change Strategies with Bernard Lonergan's Method*. Lanham, MD: University Press of America, 2014.

Remen, Rachel. "Helping, Fixing, or Serving?" https://www.mentalhealthsf.org/wp-content/uploads/2020/01/HelpingFixingServing-by-Rachel-Remen.pdf.

Ricoeur, Paul. *Essays on Biblical Interpretation*. Edited by Lewis Mudge. Philadelphia: Fortress, 1980.

———. *Finitude et culpabilite, II, La symbolique du mal*. Paris: Aubier, 1960.

Rose-Wiles, Lisa. "The Functional Specialties: A Workshop on Applying Lonergan." Proceedings of the Praxis Program of the Advanced Seminar on Mission's Third Annual Summer Workshop, Trieste, Italy, July 24–27, 2017. https://scholarship.shu.edu/cgi/viewcontent.cgi?article=1000&context=praxis-proceedings.

Sant, Joseph. "Mendel, Darwin and Evolution." http://www.scientus.org/Mendel-Darwin.html.

Shah, Premal, and Deborah Mountain. "The Medical Model Is Dead—Long Live the Medical Model." *The British Journal of Psychiatry* 191 (2007) 375–77.

Shute, Michael. "Functional Collaboration as the Implementation of 'Lonergan's Method' Part 1: For What Problem Is Functional Collaboration the Solution?" *Journal of Macrodynamics Analysis* 8 (2015) 67–92.

———. *The Origins of Lonergan's Notion of the Dialectic of History: A Study of Lonergan's Early Writings on History*. Lanham, MD: University Press of America, 1993.

———. "Two Fundamental Notions of Economic Science." *The Lonergan Review* 2.1 (2010) 95–106.

Simpson, Jim. "Normal Wasn't Working: Economic Justice in a Post-COVID Reality." *Sojourners Magazine*, May 5, 2020. https://sojo.net/articles/normal-wasnt-working-economic-justice-post-covid-reality.

Skyttner, Lars. *General Systems Theory: Problems, Perspectives, Practice*. Singapore: World Scientific Press, 2006.

Steyn, H. C. "The Influence of Buddhism on Thomas Merton." *Journal for the Study of Religion* 3.2 (1990) 3–13.

Sulmasy, Daniel P. "A Biopsychosocial-Spiritual Model for the Care of Patients at the End of Life." *The Gerontologist* 42.3 (2002) 24–33.

———. "Diseases and Natural Kinds." *Theoretical Medicine and Bioethics* 26 (2005) 487–513.

"Systems Medicine and Healthcare Systems." www.bcsss.org/research/fields-and-groups/systems-medicine-and-healthcare-systems.

Tan, Audrey. "How Climate Change Is Linked to Virus Response." *The Strait Times*, April 25, 2020. https://www.straitstimes.com/singapore/health/how-climate-change-is-linked-to-virus-response.

Tetreault, Martine, et al. "Whole-exome Sequencing as a Diagnostic Tool: Current Challenges and Future Opportunities." *Expert Review of Molecular Diagnostics* 15.6 (2015) 1–12.

Thomasma, David C. "Anti-Foundationalism and the Possibility of a Moral Philosophy of Medicine." *Theoretical Medicine* 18 (1997) 127–43.

Tracy, David, *The Achievement of Bernard Lonergan*. New York: Herder & Herder, 1970.

———. "Method as Foundation for Theology: Bernard Lonergan's Option." *The Journal of Religion* 50.3 (1970) 292–318.

"Traditional Medicine and Surgery in Asia: China." https://www.britannica.com/science/history-of-medicine/China.

Voegelin, Eric. *Order and History*. Vol. 1, *Israel and Revelation*. Baton Rouge: Louisiana State University, 1956.

Vogt, Henrik, et al. "The New Holism: P4 Systems Medicine and the Medicalization of Health and Life Itself." *Medicine, Healthcare Philosophy* 19.2 (2016) 307–23.

Walmsley, Gerard. *Lonergan on Philosophic Pluralism: The Polymorphism of Consciousness as the Key to Philosophy*. Toronto: University of Toronto, 2008.

Wells, Jonathan. "Coronavirus, Intelligent Design, and Evolution." *Evolution News and Science Today*, March 30, 2020. https://evolutionnews.org/2020/03/coronavirus-intelligent-design-and-evolution/.

———. *The Politically Incorrect Guide to Darwinism and Intelligent Design*. Washington, DC: Regnery, 2006.

Werkmeister, W. H. *Theories of Ethics*. Lincoln, NE: Johnsen, 1961.

"What Is Wrong with Modern Medicine?" https://www.healthdom.com/what-is-wrong-with-modern-medicine/.

Whelan, Gerald. *Redeeming History: Social Concern in Bernard Lonergan and Robert Doran*. Rome: Gregorian and Biblical, 2013.

Whitehead, Alfred North. *Religion in the Making*. New York: Meridian, 1960.

Wilkins, Jeremy. *Before Truth: Lonergan, Aquinas, and the Problem of Wisdom*. Washington, DC: Catholic University of America Press, 2018.

Willich, Stefan N. "The Advent of 'E-Healthcare.'" *Medical Challenges for the New Millennium* (2001) 73–95.

Selective Subject Index

AIRR, the four levels of the transcendental imperatives, 27, 29, 33, 97
Arendt, Hannah, viii
Aquinas, St. Thomas, 23, 59, 84, 87, 88, 99
Aristotle, 19, 23, 66, 82, 87, 88, 100

Bartlett, Jonathan, 51, 119
Bateson, Gregory, 76, 119
Bateson, William, 53
Bernstein, Richard J., 66, 67, 119
Bion, Wilfred, 113, 119
Biopsychosocial model (BPS) 10, 12, 13, 15
Byrne, Patrick, xiv, 12, 129

Clinical Practice, 3, 16, 75, 96, 121
Crysdale, Cynthia, 93, 120
Cybernetics, 94, 95, 121

Daly, Patrick, ix, x, xiv, 1, 2, 4, 7, 8, passim
Daly's "GEM Model," ix, x , xv, 1,-4, 6–9, 12, 13, 15, passim
Darwin, Charles, 49, 52, 54, 71
Darwinism, xiv, 54
Doran, Robert, 13, 35, 38, 77, 84, 123
Dunne, Tad, 28, 77, 92, 120
Dysfunctions, xiv, 1, 5–7, 96

Einstein, Albert, 2, 24
Engel, George, 10, 13, 15
Eye of love, importance of, 38, 80, 110

Faith, deeper roots of, 82
Fenton, Aron, 54, 121
Francis, Pope, xiv, 55, 67, 121
Frattaroli, Elio, 5, 121
Functional Specialties, ix, xii, xiii, 4, 6, passim

Gadamer, Hans-Georg, 115, 116, 121
Generalized Empirical Method (GEM), 1, 3, 9, 25, passim
Generalized Empirical Method, Functionally Specialized (GEM-FS) 3, 6, 9, 25, passim

Healthcare, ix, x. 1, 3, 4, 7 passim
Heuristic, its characteristics in Lonergan, 23, 35, 73, 86, 105, 108
Higher viewpoint, 3
Horizon, its varied usages in Lonergan, 4, 13, 31, 41, 56
Husserl, Edmund, 16, 19, 20 23–25, 72, 122

Integrations, need of higher forms of, 27, 34, 62, 63,96. 110, 112, 113

Selective Subject Index

Interiority, importance of, 4, 25, 57, 61, passim

Jenner, Edward, 51

Kant, Immanuel, 6, 23, 24, 60. 82, 88
Kierkegaard, Soren, 67, 83 112
King, Catherine, 101, 122

Lamb, Matthew, 32, 122
Lonergan, Bernard, vii, ix, xiv, 9, passim

McCarthy, Michael, 59, 60, 124
McDonald, Marie Josephine, 77, 124
McShane, Phil, 7, 30, 71, 124
McWhinney, Ian R. 13, 15, 16, 124
Mead, Margaret, 94, 95, 124
Mediated Phase in the last four FS, 26, 30, passim
Mediating Phase in the first four FS, 6, 11, 26, 27, passim
Medicine, its various aspects, ix, 1, 3, 4 passim
Mendel, Gregor, 49, 51, 52, 54, 59
Monod, Jacques, 54
Morelli, Elizabeth, 63, 68, 124
Morelli, Mark, 11,16, 63, 68, 124,
mRNA, 28, 53, 81, 82

Operator, as used by Lonergan, 21, 35, 57, 61, 62

Pandemic, xiv, 6–8, 19, 39, 45, 51, 78–81
Plato, 74, 100
Post-Mendelian, 59
Praxis, 32, 62, 66, 67, 69
Process approach in Lonergan's method as relevant to medicine and evolution, x 2–4, 6–15, passim
Pulchalski, Christina, 89, 125

Rahner, Karl, 38, 84, 125
Raymaker, John, ix, 9, 75, 125
Ricoeur, Paul, 20, 125

SARS-CoV-2, 50, 51
Smith, W. Cantwell, 82
Systemic, 5, 7, 9, 16. 69, 90, 94
Systemic-systematic differences, 5, 90

Teilhard de Chardin, Pierre xiv, 54, 55
Transcendental imperatives, 27
Transformational Horizon, 41
Transformative Process Method devised by Lonergan, 23, 30, passim
Transition points in approaching functional specialization, xiii, 18, 38, 48, 54, 59 62 passim

Whalon, Bishop Pierre, vii

www.ingramcontent.com/pod-product-compliance
Lightning Source LLC
Chambersburg PA
CBHW072151160426
43197CB00012B/2334